WHEN A FATHER
IS HARD TO HONOR

Elva McAllaster

BRETHREN PRESS
Elgin, Illinois

When a Father is Hard to Honor

Copyright © 1984 by Brethren Press

Brethren Press, 1451 Dundee Avenue, Elgin, IL 60120

Cover design by Kathy Kline

Photo: Robert Wilson

Edited by Leslie R. Keylock

Library of Congress Cataloging in Publication Data

McAllaster, Elva, 1922-
    When a father is hard to honor.

    1. Fathers and sons. 2. Conflict of generations. 3. Ten command-
ments—Parents. 4. Youth—Religious life. I. Title.
HQ756.M385 1984   306.8'742   84-16753
ISBN O-87178-930-2 (pbk.)

Printed in the United States of America

To

    Jerry

        and Hal

           and Delbert

              and Lee

                and Joel

                  and George

                    and David

                      and Roy

                        and Kent

and the others . . .

CONTENTS

Foreword by Joe Bayly 7
Certain Gratitudes 9
Preface 11
For Eavesdroppers Only: A Further Preface 15
1. Communication Zero 17
2. Concerning Kent's Sister Katherine; Also Concerning Susan
   and Mary Jane and Karen and Connie 24
3. The Prevalence of Pain 30
4. Only One Verb 34
5. His Son, Not His Puppet 38
6. To Covet a Father 43
7. I Wish He Wouldn't 45
8. To Keep a Silence? 55
9. To Borrow a Father 58
10. To Honor Is to Forgive 62
11. To Honor Which Father? 66
12. A Cup of Subtle Poison 70
13. A Word from the Night 75
14. To Change the Filters? 80
15. When Your Mother Makes It Harder 84
16. What Would It Mean for Craig? 92
17. Address Unknown 96
18. When You Tell God about Him 103
19. To Keep on Hoping 107
20. During a Twilight 111
21. Through the Deparenting Process 113
22. You and Biff Loman 118
23. Your Other—and Unfailing—Father 123
24. Résumés, Reminders, Realisms, Reachings 127
25. From Thunder, Fire, and Earthquake 132

FOREWORD

In recent years many counselors seem to have latched onto parents as the whipping boys for all later emotional problems.

Within my reach as I write these lines is the copy of a venomous, blaming letter written by a young, professedly Christian man to his mother. I feel sure it was at the instigation of his psychiatrist. Knowing the mother, a sweet and gentle woman, from the time she was younger than her son's present age, I cannot agree with the counselor's assessment of blame.

At the opposite extreme, some religious leaders during these same years have taught that parent-child problems will be solved if only the child—who may be a single twenty- or thirty-year-old—will only obey the parents. This blame focused on the son's or daughter's duty to obey is a corollary to the blame for marital problems focused by these same leaders on the wife's failure to submit to her husband.

In this book Dr. Elva McAllaster steers a steady course between both sandbars. She therefore doesn't get beached but skillfully brings her readers to the Christian answer to parent-child problems, especially those that involve the father.

The title *When a Father is Hard to Honor* should not imply that the book is only for sons and daughters. Dr. McAllaster's wise advice provides a guide, a checklist for parents as well—at least for those who want to experience the supreme joy of Dr. Albert Schweitzer's father when the world renowned organist and missionary doctor wrote, "My father is my dearest friend." That checklist speaks throughout the book but shouts from one of the final chapters, "Your Other—and Unfailing—Father." If we husbands are to love our wives "as Christ also loved the church," we are surely to love our daughters and sons as our heavenly Father loves us.

The commandment "Honor your father" takes on fresh lustre as the author distinguishes between honor and trust, honor and obey, honor and like—even honor and respect. Here and throughout the book Dr. McAllaster stresses principles, usually illustrating them from her experience over many years of teaching and relating to young men and women at Seattle Pacific University and Greenville College. When, toward the book's end, she addresses readers as "my dears," you know she means it, especially if you're a hurting son or daughter.

The book is practical. What about the son who has dropped out, whose parents' letters are returned to them marked "Address Unknown"? How shall children respond to a mother who constantly downgrades their father? To a divorced scoundrel of a father? To a father who travels a lot? (Try establishing a tradition: "[Play] the triumphal march from Aida whenever Dad comes home from a business trip.") Are "substitute fathers" good or bad? What is "deparenting" and how should sons and daughters respond when parents resist the idea —even after their children have established their own homes?

A fillip to the book's urgent content is provided by Dr. McAllaster's background as a professor of English. From Plato to Shakespeare to Arthur Miller's *Death of a Salesman*, she provides excellent literary illustrations. I especially appreciated her sympathetic treatment of Biff, Willie Loman's son.

The grace of God is a pervasive theme throughout the book—pervasive and radiant.

Like Flannery O'Connor, another Christian writer, whose life was confined to a narrow place because of her illness, Elva McAllaster's years have largely been confined to a small midwestern college town. But like Miss O'Connor, Miss McAllaster has understood and embraced a world of hurting young men and women who represent many generations of students.

Few books will have the impact of this one on the maturing family if sons and daughters, mothers and fathers will only read it.

I sincerely hope they will.

Joseph Bayly
Bartlett, Illinois

CERTAIN GRATITUDES

This book has been in progress, in one way and another, for a dozen years, and more. My gratitude goes out to those who have made its completion now possible. Particularly, I am grateful to the administration of Greenville College for the freedom to work on it intensively during a January interterm, and to the college trustees for awarding me a sabbatical during which some of the final writing was done.

I am deeply grateful to all the persons whose experiences and conversations have fed my mind and stirred my yearnings toward the enterprise; I could not begin to name them all—and it would not be appropriate to try, since too much was too confidential.

Specific appreciations can be joyfully mentioned:

. . . To Bill Chickering. While he was an editor at Christian Herald Books (and while that firm was a publisher of books), Bill helped me initiate this version of the project. He provided many helpful comments, observations, and suggestions.

. . . To Leslie H. Stobbe, formerly the editorial director in the same office, for both his enthusiastic encouragement and specific ideas he helpfully nudged me to incorporate.

. . . To Dr. Mathias Zahniser, who read many manuscript pages and gave me useful commentaries while he was a colleague at Greenville College.

. . . To a faithful student typist, Sue Park, whose cheerfulness was matched only by her skill in deciphering my tangled webs of revision thrice revised.

. . . To friends whose cordial interest and prayers strengthened my hands at crucial times in the development of the manuscript. (Especially you, Jason; especially you, Chad; especially you, Joe.)

. . . To the editors of *Christian Herald* magazine, who helped to launch the book when they adapted sections of preliminary manuscript into an article for their columns.

. . . To Leslie R. Keylock, the book editor at The Brethren Press. I appreciate the courage of his vision for Christian publishing as well as his genial grace in working with multitudinous practical details.

. . . And most of all—let me say it quietly, reverently—to my dearest Friend, my Lord, through whom and at whose command, if I'm hearing him accurately, I have turned to the typewriters.

PREFACE

As a college teacher I never know what to expect when a student taps at my office door. There may be a question about tomorrow's assignment or about last Thursday's examination or about term paper topics. Sometimes bigger items than the immediate academic ones come into view: career aptitudes, applications for graduate school, recommendations for jobs. Sometimes deep issues of personal relationships tumble to the surface. "Shall I go ahead with this interracial romance?" "I love Tom but he has traits that really bother me. Should I marry him?" "Bill and Jerry both want me to go steady. What in the world am I going to do?"

Some of the consultations are quickly spoken, quickly forgotten. Others linger and burn in the mind. While they linger, while they burn, I have to know that they represent many, many other conversations of persons far beyond my office doors. (Spoken conversations, and never-yet-spoken conversations that really need to be uttered.)

From all of my conversations with students down through my years of college teaching, one sort especially haunts me as I remember the strained, painful voices and faces of young people who are not on good terms with their fathers. In talking with my students, and with off-campus acquaintances too, I have increasingly come to believe that there is no other human stress and pain quite like the stress and pain of father/child alienation. With that belief has come an increasing sense of inner command: to say to the alienated ones, far out beyond my office walls, some of the kinds of things I try to say within these walls.

Father/child alienation comes in many sizes, shapes, and kinds, of course. It isn't all of one texture. The young people who find it very hard to comply with one phrase Moses brought back from Mt. Sinai—"Honor thy father"—have known different tensions, different provocations and embitterments.

I remember, I remember.

I remember Jerry—whose real name was not Jerry, just as any other person I mention only by a given name all through these discussions will be meeting you under a fictional name. I think about Jerry sitting at the back of my Romantic Literature classroom with his head cradled on his arms while the rest of us talked about Shelley's ideas.

(Or was it Byron's verse forms?) Although Jerry was a brilliant student, he was totally tuned out to us that day. Jerry's father was a well-known evangelical leader, honored and admired all across America, but Jerry didn't admire with the others. Jerry counted him a dictatorial tyrant and was coming to hate him with a steely, violent, and durable rage.

I think about Hal, whose parents had heckled and nagged him all through high school, he said, because they didn't see any value in his passion for music. Stereo, guitars, combos, concerts. Hal's parents wanted him to be spending his time, instead, on projects that would help him to Earn a Good Living. And his spirit still dribbled pus when I had him in class. (For one Hal whom I listened to that semester, how many thousands of hurting Hals are there out across all of America?)

I think about Delbert and the tight, angry enigma of his face when I saw him at his restaurant job. Then enigma wasn't enigma when I realized his father was one of his customers and Delbert was resenting with quiet fury his father's kind of extroverted humor among the other patrons.

Or Lee, so bored and suffocated by his parents' values and lifestyle that he moved out and dropped out.

Or Joel, who explained to me an unscheduled absence from campus: he had been called home to help his mother get his alcoholic father hospitalized after a time of prolonged drinking.

I think about George, whom I saw on the stairs in Hogue Hall just a few weeks ago. "Any time today when I could see you?" he wondered. "Some things have come up."

"How about right now?" I said. "I'm just on my way to my office."

George turned and went back up to the second floor with me, closed the door of my office, told me about the "things" that had "come up." We discussed this alternative, and this, and this. "Have you talked it all over with your folks?" I asked after a time.

George shook his head. "I can't talk about these things at home," he said in a pinched and quiet voice.

I remember David, who told me ruefully how he and his father could converse for half an hour at a time and then realize that neither had really understood one thing the other had expressed. Not one thing.

I glance at a sheaf of photos here beside me in a wide black ceramic bowl where Christmas card photographs and other snapshots have been accumulating. Roy, several years beyond my classrooms and laughing blithely now in this new glimpse. Under the laughter, memory has to see the tense and bitter lines in his face when he wrote themes about his father or talked about his father. A preacher father who had deserted the pastorate and the parsonage and the PKs. During his campus days Roy lived in raw and searing agony.

Kent lives in agony, too. Kent, whom I got to know through my writing, not my teaching. "Estranged from my father," Kent has written to me. It is obvious that anger and pain and resentment were dripping through the keys as he typed. His father dallied and dallied with other women and finally divorced Kent's mother to marry a woman Kent deplores. And across these five states I reach out to grip Kent's hand. Kent's hand, and the hands of all the Kents everywhere.

Recently in a library I heard two women talking about an interesting and influential book for "hurting parents." One of them mentioned with a smile that the book had been on an end table in her home when a young visitor had picked it up and offered his opinion that there should be a parallel book, for "hurting kids."

For several years now, as I have thought about the Jerrys of America—and the Hals, the Delberts, the Lees, the Joels, the Georges, the Davids, the Roys, the Kents—that has been my increasing conviction, too: there should be a book for hurting kids.

Are you one of them?

Maybe you are not yet in college. Maybe you are far past college. Whatever your other roles, if you are one of the "hurting kids," these pages are for you.

May I come in and talk with you?

I am not a worker of magic; I can't repair relationships instantly—presto, changeo. I have often smiled with my classes about wanting a magic wand to transport them to Shakespeare's Stratford with me, or to Wordsworth's Lake District of England. I don't even have that kind of magic. Yet I have observed some principles of human experience during all the people-watching that has come along with loving and instructing college students—several thousands of them, by now, on several campuses. And I do know something about the working of Grace in human lives—and Grace is better than magic would be.

Another disclaimer, just to be sure we all know where we stand. I'm not a professional counselor, either: not a clinical psychologist, not a preacher, not one with diplomas in family practice. I come to you just as person to person, just as one who has scrutinized human beings in the literature books and loved them in daily association, as one who knows something about Grace.

Everything I say won't speak equally to everyone; shall we assume that at the outset? (Hal isn't Delbert, and Delbert isn't George.) Some of you are in a new and sudden spurt of anger since a quarrel last night about car keys; some of you have lived with rages and resentments ever since your high school times. If one of these pages doesn't come in on your wave length, will you try another? And another? Please? I hope you will keep listening, even when I make you angry for a while.

Because I care, very deeply, about the hurting kids . . . .

FOR EAVESDROPPERS ONLY:
A FURTHER PREFACE

Yes, I hope you *will* listen in on these conversations!

If you are pastor or parent or counselor or friend to the people I am talking with, I hope you will listen in. I hope with a yearning intensity that you will pick up some ideas, attitudes, perspectives, and anecdotes here that can help you to be helpful as you interact with your Jerry or Delbert or Joel or Kent.

Many topics and principles that have had to be on my mind while I wrote these essays will resonate, I hope, in far wider circles of human experience, as well as in the filial circumstances that have evoked them. I shall be very joyful if things I am saying to Jerry or Joel can be useful also in marital relationships, among siblings, in friendships, in employer-employee contexts, in pastor-parish contexts—among counselors of any sort, any at all.

Especially—oh, most especially—I venture to hope you may do some eavesdropping if you are a father. There might be reinforcements here that you will value as you notice pitfalls you have avoided. There might be ideas here that you could transpose, ideas that will help you reach out toward the son who needs you. Possibly, possibly, you have been harder to honor, sometimes, than you might have dreamed, and listening in on these conferrings might be for you and yours "a means of Grace." If so, I shall be immeasurably glad.

Especially, also, I hope your eavesdropping will be useful if you are a girl or woman who has turned to this book because *your* father has been hard to honor. (Are you a Jeri, a Della, a Joan, a Georgette, rather than a Jerry, a Delbert, a Joel, a George?) In hearing the inner summonses to write this book as it is, I have not been unaware that daughters also have their needs. I have, in fact, included as chapter 2 an essay particularly dedicated to you, and I truly hope you can sift through the various other essays and find some principles that fit your exact shoe size.

During all the years this book has been rooting and sprouting and growing in the orchards of my mind, I have felt strongly that it needed the creative unity of one voice discussing one segment of human experience, but I hope most earnestly and pray devoutly that the fruit here harvested can also nourish a good many other kinds of hunger.

To anyone at all who can use it in any way whatsoever: please do so!

Perhaps you will like to do collective eavesdropping. Adult Sunday school classes or women's study groups or P.T.A-type fellowships may want to listen in together and talk with each other about what they hear.

For such group listening, as well as for the individual listener, perhaps I should mention that I have thought of the various essays as separate entities, so they can be read in any order whatsoever. This is not a novel with a chronological plot to be followed in sequence!

Let me reiterate my invitation to anyone at all who can use this book in any way whatsoever: please do so. And may blessings upon blessings attend each use, through Him.

1

COMMUNICATION ZERO

Have you ever driven across prairie roads just after a vast ice storm and seen telephone wires drooping in wide scallops or dangling in broken, mournful pieces? Have you picked up a telephone in a home served by those wires and heard blank nothing? Have you sent off letters and had them come back stamped in purple ink "Undeliverable. Return to Sender"?

Since the time of smoke signals and the pony express, since the time of beacons blazed across Greek mountains to signal the end of the Trojan wars, since the time of conversations in Eden, communication has been important among human beings—and communication has had its ways of breaking down. Ice builds up; wires sag lower and lower. Finally, zin-n-n-ng, and a wire snaps and sways uselessly in the blizzards.

It won't be news to you that communication between a father and a son is often especially fragile, and that sometimes it comes to the horrible zin-n-n-ng of complete breakdown. Not always, of course, and we thank the Lord for that. Two days ago I was a guest at an open house, and in the midst of diverse and lively conversation, our host's bearded son, home from his university courses, had an occasion to tell me with a wide grin, "My father and I have been on good terms since I was seven." He represents one big segment of humanity. But there is another segment, to whom his easy rapport is just a stab of sharper pain in the midst of always-lived-with pain. And it's you, in the latter segment, with whom I am now conversing.

Candidly, what is your level of communication with your father right now? What has it been in the past two weeks, the past six months? On a continuum of one to ten, would it hover somewhere around a three, or a 1.5? Or is it right now firmly stuck on zero? For a good many fellows in contemporary America "zero" would have to be the honest answer.

I look out the window, watching dry maple leaves ripple and sway in the tree beyond my study. While literal eyes watch them and watch a blue jay dip-soar past, my other eyes watch some of the fellows I know. I see broken wires. Telephones out of order. Dead-letter purple ink.

Tom. Unless there's new news I haven't heard, he has not spoken more than three sentences to his father in the past three years. And what he spoke last was in the flaming anger of repudiation.

Matthew. When I talked with his father a few days ago, big Matthew didn't even know young Matthew's present address. Somewhere downtown, in their town.

Otis. He was my student several years ago, and I remember poignantly his comment when he brought back my copy of C. S. Lewis's *Letters to Malcolm*. It had given him an idea, Otis said. He was going to try writing some letters to his father, as Lewis had written to Malcolm. Otis was living and working only a few miles from home and had meals with his family rather often, but his father never seemed to hear him when they talked, he said; not really to hear.

Roy. Chatting with Roy's mother once when I was in their town, I told her blithely about my gladness in some of Roy's ideas for creative writing. "If he would just write *letters!*" she said with a quiet intensity that almost made me feel I had been bruising her whole body while I chattered.

Johnny. He's living under his father's roof, and yet he is not. He's a six-foot owl, without feathers, working or prowling by night and sleeping by day. In that way he avoids conversations he can't cope with. On a given day his mother would tell you, "Where's the ketchup?" might be his total attempt at conversation. Or he might mumblegrumble, "Was there any mail?" or "Where did you put my gray sweater?" His tones of voice always tell his parents that the telephone lines are down—and the blizzards still blowing.

Chad. His father lives in another state and becomes daily more estranged from him. Christmas cards still go back and forth, or a postcard now and then, but "Love, Dad" in the signatures is a travesty and "Love, Chad" is a hypocrisy.

Back to *you*, and I wonder again. Communication zero? Or 1.5? On a good weekend, up to three?

When real communication is not present among relatives, psychic pain is always present. ("You're telling *me*?" Chad would ask scornfully. "That's the understatement of the decade!" he would fling through stiffened throat muscles. "Psychic pain? And *how!*" Okay. Stay with me, Chad. And please listen to this, Chad. Some time ago I read a wise word from the hand of Jay Kesler in *Campus Life* magazine. It's regrettably true, he observed, that often the initiative must come from the young person if youth-parent communication is to be improved. Must. Are you listening? Things can be better than they are, but only if *you* do something about it.

Probably, in that case, a first thing to do is to ponder about some whys and wherefores.)

What went wrong, then, to keep you from being like that bearded university student who has been on good terms with his father ever since he was seven?

Try these for size?

. . . You don't really want to have open channels between you, because what came through would be his disapproval of your lifestyle. He doesn't like your friends, your hobbies, your music, your habits, your anything. If you open up to him, you're making yourself vulnerable to reproof and unwanted advice. And that hurts.

. . . He has always been so preoccupied with his job and his clubs and his civic activities that a real conversation with you has seldom happened.

. . . He holds his opinions too strongly to hear, really hear, any of yours. (Politics? Pacifism? Race relations? Church? Your aptitudes? Your summer plans?)

. . . He travels a lot for his work, and when he is at home he seems to be engrossed in catching up on everything but you.

. . . He doesn't ever seem to sense a need for letting you know what he is thinking, even when it concerns your welfare or your future.

I pause to watch a small convention of grackles out in the maple tree, in the dry grass, winging away. They're almost as synchronized as a ballet corps. I watch the elegant white tips of blue wings as another jay dip-soars past. And I am listening again to an alert, intense young professional woman as she confided her aching wish: that Dad would let her and her brothers in on more of his thinking, more of his planning. This trip for this summer he would decide, and they, startled, would unmake and remake their assorted plans and expectations. This college for you. No, this college for you. Your tasks for this weekend; this, and this, and this. Your mother and I are going to XYZ and you will stay with ABC while we are gone. No, that is what I have decided, Catherine; there's no need to discuss it. When we talked, Catherine was half-angry, half-amused, and altogether vexed. From what she said then, I gathered that her brothers' reactions were sharper than hers. Psychic pain.

. . . He feels strange inside your world. He seems to fumble and grope.

He was uncomfortable at P.T.A. when you were seven, maybe? He seemed perplexed by the activities and events that high school required of you? And anything you mention of your college experience seems to be like a report on flying saucers to baffle him?

. . . You have experienced isolation and detachment, isolation and detachment, until now it's hard to break through anywhere.

Another quick recollection. Hal greeted me when I was coming from the campus one afternoon and escorted me to my front door, talking with slow pain about his emotional turmoils. Invited into my living room, he talked on and on and on. At one point I asked whether he had shared these turmoils at home. Hal shook his head quickly. "It's as though I were three people," he said, "and my parents know only one of me."

. . . He isn't easily verbal in personal communication. Especially when emotions go deep, he tends to move off like a big elk or moose disturbed in its feeding and needing the dark-shadowed forest.

. . . In your family the tendency has always been not to talk something through until it becomes a crisis. Then tempers flare and Dad shouts ultimatums and Mom cries. And you are left feeling like a criminal in court. Right?

Have you found the size of your shoulders in one of these garments we have been pulling from the racks? Don't hesitate to keep on looking. The more accurately you can understand yourself and Dad, the better your chances of shaking the ice off the telephone wires.

It may be that Dad is actually longing to change the rating scale, too. Maybe he would like, even more earnestly than you would, to see the indicator move from Communication Zero up to 1.5 or 4.5 or seven or nine.

How to do it? How to do it?

Again, shall we go shopping and see what fits your brawny shoulders? Will you tug on this tweed? Or this plaid?

. . . Have you taken him out for a meal lately, or for coffee? Might you? Just the two of you? Father's Day might offer a convenient occasion, if it's near at hand, or his birthday, or some other holiday. Otherwise, maybe you could blithely suggest that it's time you paid him back for some of the sleep he lost through your infant squallings and colic and diapers and burpings!

. . . Can you watch for things to do with him? On weekends if you're still at home, on vacations if you're off at college or employed away from home, can you set up opportunities for incidental conversation while paintbrushes dip and swing, while moist earth is turned by spades, while leaves get burned and cars get washed? Do you ever hunt with him, fish with him, play golf with him? No? Well, might you begin?

Once upon a Saturday a student stopped at my front door to leave an assignment. He apologized for looking wind-blown and bedraggled, and explained that he had been out hunting deer with his father since 3:30 that morning. "Any luck?" I asked. He shrugged ruefully. Not one deer. Not this year, and not for the past several years. "Is it worth it, getting up so early, and out in all that cold, and coming back empty-handed?" He shrugged. "Well, Dad likes to go. It's about the only time to be with him, really. Hunting or fishing." I'm glad, glad, glad that Bill is willing to get up at 3:30 on a Saturday morning in mid-December.

In an earlier era fathers and sons often worked together, as you well know, on their farms or in small family businesses. There were built-in opportunities for talking over the heart-huge topics. Now we may have to make appointments for any of Dad's time and scheme cunningly in order to paint the back porch with him or do an errand two towns away with him. It's worth the scheming!

. . . If your world seems rather foreign to him, can you keep breaking open peepholes for him to see through? Do you let him see your themes and term papers? Do you send him clippings about the town where you are working? Do you write an occasional paragraph about your boss, your newest roommate, your latest concert-going, your next trip to the mountains?

. . . Can you keep sending out signals of a sort that do not threaten his emotional balance nor even require a direct response, of an "I-want-to-keep-in-touch-with-you" sort?

Have you recently mailed a postcard to his business address? Maybe it carries only a few words ("I love you, Dad; have a good day") and your initials. Maybe it alludes to that best vacation ever when you were eight or nine and brings a new smile to you and to him.

. . . In any family some topics tend to become explosive. (Curfew hours? Grades? The vocation he expects you to follow? Local politics?) Can you sometimes, often, be wary of those red-flag topics and build rapport by talking with him in more and more depth on the safer topics?

Can you try to find out, for example, what he really thinks on some ecology issue? Can you induce him to reminisce about his first jobs, about Great-Granddad's days as a cowboy, about his GI experiences?

Can you borrow an idea or two from Alex Haley and let Dad tell you what he knows about your own roots?

. . . Can you make overtures toward talking things through before they move to crisis stages?

One can't always predict, of course, but some open comments on Thursday and Saturday about your Sunday plans might keep violence from erupting on Sunday when your plans crash head-on against his plans. To mention tentative thoughts about changing a major or colleges or jobs while the thoughts are still filmy-thin and nebulous might prepare the way for quiet, rational decisions rather than shouting matches when the new semester begins. Might?

. . . Have you recently had the courage to offer an apology when conscience kept summoning you so to do?

Did you speak to him in anger and squeal your tires at the corner as you drove away, and then come home in dour silence? Did you mumble a surly "Good morning" over breakfast eggs for the next week but never look Dad in the face and say a "Sorry" to him?

It's still profoundly true, as it was in the time of wise old King Solomon, that the soft answer "turneth away wrath" and that "grievous words stir up anger." (I'm looking at Proverbs 15:1.) Has your father become quite unaccustomed to the soft answer from you? Then how about starting a precedent?

. . . If you tend to wince against scoldings and unwelcome advice that might buffet you if you were more open to him, could you develop a wholesome objectivity by making a small game with yourself and pretending that you are collecting material to put into a book about him sometime? Rather than just boiling up with emotion, could you notice carefully what he says and how, and then jot down bits of his tirades in a journal? In small measure could you imitate James Boswell keeping notes on the views and foibles of Dr. Samuel Johnson, back in the eighteenth century?

Actually, some day—who knows?—you might like to have such jottings available when you come to write your autobiography. Or you might turn out to be a clever chap like Clarence Day, whose rollicking reminiscences, *Life with Father*, amused literate America when they appeared in print. His father's eccentricities and ego and tempestuous wrath could not have been easy to live with when Clarance Day was a youngster, but he obviously stored recollections away with objectivity and amusement and later earned a good many shekels by having done so.

Even if you're utterly remote from being a budding Clarence Day, do keep in mind that describing something in a journal can help you keep poised and objective and amused, rather than angry or embittered, about whatever you describe. That I know well from all my own journalizing experiences. Will it help your emotional equilibrium to give journal-keeping a try?

Shall I hope you will be trying experiments like all of these and a great many others?

I can't make full predictions nor give guarantees, of course. All that you have ever said to him since your first little wailing yelps from your bassinet are a part of the communication networks, or communication barriers, in the present eras in your life. But within the measurings of Grace, "hitherto" is never the measure nor the limit of "henceforward," and the indicator on the communication rating scale can change in times to come.

2

CONCERNING KENT'S SISTER KATHERINE; ALSO CONCERNING SUSAN AND MARY JANE AND KAREN AND CONNIE

As I drove home from Carlyle Lake last evening, thoughts about Kent's sister Katherine kept imprinting themselves over the scenes of Illinois silos and Illinois Holstein herds, over new green wheat, oak woods, low gray clouds.

Katherine.

I haven't met her, but what Kent has written burns in my mind. It's evident that Kent's anger and pain about his father is both embittered and compounded because Kent can't help seeing what his father has done to Katherine's morale. Has done and is doing. For these several years now—during Dad's extra-marital affairs, the divorce, his remarriage, his continuing tendency to ignore his children—Katherine has known searing hurt, rejection, anger, dismay.

What if, I ask myself. What if Katherine and Kent had been in the car behind me when I swung around that loaded corn wagon on Highway 127 last evening? What if they had turned right at Idler Lane when I did and followed my Plymouth up Elm Street to Beaumont and come into my very living room to talk for a while?

If Kent had wanted to wander over to explore the Greenville College campus, what might I have said to Katherine while he was away? Or if Kent had come alone, asking me how he can counsel Katherine, what would I tell him?

Well, partly I'd just reiterate a good many of the ideas I affirm all through these pages. "Communication Zero" and puppetry and the rest apply to girls, too, and not just to guys. Sometimes such topics may be easier for Katherine to catch hold of than for Kent. (For all the Katherines, for a Katherine and a Susan and a Mary Jane, for a Karen and a Connie and a thousand others. For girls with fathers who are hard to honor.) Sometimes girls find it easier to be tolerant and forgiving and flexible and accepting toward the dismaying father than their brothers do. For a girl there may be a degree of detachment, faintly parallel with the way she can watch a neighbor's misdeeds and not feel herself responsible nor threatened when Dad shows himself weak or erring. Sometimes the Katherines are more resiliently able to keep putting Dad back on a pedestal than the Kents are.

But let's face your present situation, Katherine. I'm glad you are here with Kent. Your being with him leads to an opener we ought to establish right away. It's this: since their perceptions of any episode or any trait may vary, it's often a good, good thing if siblings can talk candidly and honestly with each other about what is happening to them and in them. Talked-about emotions are often clarified emotions; often, too, they become emotions brought more readily into balance.

In homes in which respect for parents has been enforced but not always deserved, depth-level discussions may help to free both the Kents and the Katherines from guilt feelings they should not be carrying. While I murmur that principle, I think of a woman I know who might tell you (if she were confiding at deep enough levels) how very freeing she found it when her wise brother told her meditatively, "We might as well face it; our mother has a persecution complex." Dutifully reluctant even to phrase criticisms of a parent in her mind, Mrs. J. had been harboring too much self-reproach for her own inner health, along with the inescapable too-much of vexation toward a parent. And Mrs. J. would represent many, many others.

So talk things over with Katherine, Kent! Talk things over with Kent, Katherine! Each of you may gain a new awareness that will be helpful and healing—eventually if not immediately.

When we consider specific suggestions for ways to honor Dad or open up the conduits of communication, there will, of course, be a great deal of overlapping on "his" and "hers" lists; what I'm nudging the Kents to try, all through these discussions, the Katherines could be trying also. (The Susans, the Mary Janes, the Karens, the Connies.) But do keep in mind, girls, that every human equation is different from every other; a father-daughter connection is precious, and special, and never exactly duplicated in the whole wide earth. I thought about that fact last night when—with Katherine very much in my mind—I sat in a church pew behind a young father and watched his four-year-old daughter's confidings, cuddlings, and adorings all through a church service. Daughters are unique and special to fathers; fathers are unique and special to daughters.

"So?" queries Katherine, cocking a carefully shaped and pretty brown eyebrow.

So, my dear, your father will always have emotional needs that are precisely *your* size. Whatever attention he gets from sons or colleagues or a second family, there's a Katherine-shaped space in his heart. It may be cluttered with a lot of emotional debris right now, but it's there. He needs *your* love, *your* attention, *your* concern, *your* solicitude.

Maybe most of all he needs your forgiving. (Try the stress both ways: he needs *your* forgiving; he needs your *forgiving*.) He may never ask for it; he may be like the kinds of untempered steel that will break before they can bend. But he needs your forgiveness, both retroactive, for all that has happened up to now, and renewed, for today's mail (or the lack of it) and tomorrow's telephoned words (or telephone silences). He needs to be forgiven.

And you need to forgive him, Katherine. For your own inner poise and grace and growth. For your rapport with all the other men you encounter and will encounter, you need to forgive him. You see, in the whole sensitive network that makes up human personality, a woman's attitudes toward her father are exceedingly consequential. Exceedingly. If we could tune in on the offices of pastors, psychologists, psychiatrists, and other counselors all across America at this precise moment, you can be sure we would hear a good many versions of "I hated my father, and now I cannot—cannot—truly love my husband. Help me!"

Just here, you see, is a way that God's ancient promise attached to the sixth of the Ten Commandments is very relevant to contemporary America. The Israelites were told to honor their parents in order that "it may go well with thee, in the land which the Lord thy God giveth thee." (That's Deuteronomy 5:16) The principle from Sinai still applies broadly in human affairs: people honor parents and things go well with them, people dishonor parents and things crack apart. A girl cherishes unforgiving angers toward her father and finds them to be snake eggs inside her when she dates, is courted, marries.

Just a few days ago I had a long letter from a thoughtful Christian leader who wanted me to know about a counselee of his; her story cries "Katherine! Katherine! Katherine!" in my mind. In brief, his counselee had been through dark teen-age rebellion and continuing hatred toward Dad, and she is now needing help for the emotional paralysis of her marriage.

And more may be paralyzed than your masculine friendships or a courtship or a marriage while "I hate Dad" is a malignant tumor within your spirit. We can't rightly use the same tongue, wrote St. James (I'm looking at chapter 3 of his epistle and verse 9), to bless God and to "curse men, which are made after the similitude of God." If cursing mankind in general "ought not so to be," how much more poisonous to the Godward relationship is continuing hatred toward one's very father!

To experience pain is not sin; let's be clear about that. But to cherish resentment and hatred against the pain-giver—"Ay, there's the rub." (Mr. Hamlet said it; a friend of yours, perhaps?) And until it's cut away by the Surgeon, that sin-tumor can send infection all through your Christian life, your vocational plans, your goals, your very destiny.

I'm thinking now of Elizabeth, a vivacious jokester I once had in a writing class. My first real clue that she was in deep trouble (with herself, with God, and with her strongly-felt missionary call) came when she wrote a bitter little poem about the lure of suicide. Well, the Surgeon performed operations, and Elizabeth did become a missionary, not a suicide. One of the surgeries dealt with a grim, big, leathery sac full of her hate-resentment-anger emotions toward her unpleasant stepfather.

Let's probe another realism.

You can't make Dad into a dream father by willing him to be so, Katherine. You cannot erase the grim events that have happened. His folly is still folly. His old tyranny may still be tyranny, although with more maturity you just may be ready to use a different word for it. You may not change one of his habits or one of his attitudes, even though you pray desperately and make uncounted overtures. Ultimately you are not responsible for his uses of his life—but you are responsible for your uses of your life. And in order that things may "go well" with you in the deep, deep levels of your being, Katherine, you need to forgive.

When I said "dream father" a moment ago, did I touch a raw nerve?

Ever since the first post-Eden women watched their menfolk handle animals or handle weapons or handle governments, girls have wanted to admire their fathers. Have wished, yearned, been wistful; have earnestly desired. It's deep inside you: "He's my Dad, and I want him to be my hero, too."

Katherine nods and shrugs. "So how can I function when I *cannot* admire him? When I don't even respect him?"

I pick up a ceramic paperweight and twiddle with it. Rapid thoughts. Half a silent prayer. Look, Katherine. Look ahead to what I say later about "only one verb." I think it applies, and crucially, to your situation. You would like to admire; that's natural and understandable. But the sixth Sinai command has only one verb: you are to *honor* him. You are not instructed nor required nor commanded to *admire*.

Splitting hairs? No, I don't think so. Many things would be nice in this human life that we survive without. Some things, however, are utterly basic and essential. To admire him is fine, if you can and when you can and wherein you can; to honor him is not optional in a right kind of life.

I put down the paperweight and pick up a much-used book. I flip to Philippians. Here's something that could make huge, huge differences, Katherine, in your hunger to admire and in all that relates to it. Let's try a new and very specific reading of Philippians 4:8. Like this:

> Finally, *Katherine*, whatsoever things are true *about your father*, whatsoever things are honest *in him*, whatsoever things are just, whatsoever things are pure, whatsoever things are lovely, whatsoever things are of good report; if there be any virtue *in his life*, and if there be any praise *you can give him*, think on these things.

It's the King James Version I'm adapting from at this moment; maybe you will like to read the same verse and adapt from it in half a dozen modern versions. Do notice one marginal variation here in the KJV; "honest," the margin tells us, could also be read as "venerable." That's a word to send emotion tingling along one's epidermis.

How about making a tremendous effort—maybe for the next month—to concentrate on the "any praise" elements? Before you sleep tonight get out a pencil and paper and write down the things that come to mind. At first the resentments may seem so huge you will throw down the pencil and say there are no "whatsoevers" at all—but keep thinking. And thinking. And thinking!

Maybe it will start the sequence of your rememberings and jottings and praisings if I mention a theme that came across my desk one time. A girl whose father could have been commended by his business associates for at least a hundred traits received her admiration, in that freshman paper, because of his lean, flat midriff—which he kept that way by playing golf regularly, she said. If your father has a midriff you can praise, a golf score you can value, jot those items down. If he's good with cats, or with cucumbers. If he drives a car skillfully. If he has a neat mustache. If not those, what is "of good report," by any standards whatsoever?

Now, having started to make a list of appreciations, can you do it continually? When one part of you wants to seethe "Dad is not fair to me," can another part of you quickly counter "is not" with a positive and definite "is"?

While you work on this assignment, you might like to find a copy of Erwin Lutzer's book *Managing Your Emotions* and look up the story he tells (page 41 and following) of a young woman who was startled and joyful to discover how very much her life was changed when she carried through a similar "assignment" from her pastor. Fierce hatred for her stepfather, who had abused her sexually, underwent a holy chemical process that changed her in jubilant ways.

Next thought.

Will it give you strength sometimes, Katherine, to reach out to someone who is newer in suffering than you are? In a homely metaphor: an irrigation ditch in a garden not only carries water to distant beans or beets or pumpkins; the ditch itself is never parched, dry-caked earth while water is flowing through. If you let the water of Grace flow through, you yourself will be watered earth.

And there's probably more suffering all around you than you would ever notice while your preoccupation stays with Dad's most recent callousness toward you. I caught a new perception of the prevalence of suffering once when three students came to my home to use my personal library in working on notebooks for a course project. As they worked, they chatted—and I reeled inwardly while I heard their comments. As I recall it, Girl A's parents were about to get a divorce; Girl B had acquired a new stepmother, of her own age, immediately after Dad divorced Mom; Girl C said ironically that although they couldn't stand each other, her parents got along okay because Dad worked nights and Mom worked days, and they didn't see enough of each other to fight much.

Around you at work or school or church, Katherine, there are probably some A girls or B girls or C girls. There are some who need a steadying hand and proffered kleenex and invitations toward Strength where you have found it—where you have found Him.

Katherine's pretty eyebrows go up again. "Strength? Him?" I hand her a leatherbound book from the shelf behind me, and smile. Try Psalm 46:1. It's Rx for all sorts of emergencies, including those of the "life with father" kinds.

Well, Katherine and Kent didn't drive along Route l27 last night, and there is no breath of Katherine's perfume lingering in my living room. Perhaps I shall meet her some day, perhaps I shall not. For now I'm very glad that Kent cares about his little sister's emotional stresses. I hope their concern for each other can be increasingly a tool of Grace to both. I hope that "to forgive" can become more and more of a key verb for Katherine . . . And also for Susan . . . And Mary Jane . . . And Karen . . . And Connie . . . And the rest.

3

THE PREVALENCE OF PAIN

How's this for a theorem in human affairs? *There's more youth-parent pain in our society than a lot of people know about or usually admit to.*

It's a bigger theorem than the ones you grappled with in your geometry textbooks, isn't it? Are you willing to grip hold of this consequential theorem, shake the metal it's built from, and probe its corollaries?

To consider it strenuously could be useful in quite a few ways. Think about these:

—If you are living your own life from pain-crisis to pain-crisis, to recognize that about a jillion other people struggle also may help you to keep your perspective and your equilibrium.

—We hear sometimes about a deep human principle of "the wounded healer." If you know (or have known) youth-parent pain, you may be the one who can help some of your associates in their pain times. If you are alert enough, perceptive enough to hear pain when it whimpers or moans under its breath, you can apply poultices often, often.

—If you are one who has usually walked sunny and serene paths—if you have really experienced very few emotional thunderstorms within your family—then touching this theorem may help you to reach out a sturdy hand to some of your friends who now have hailstones in their hair and soggy shoes and flapping wet garments.

—Since youth-parent tension is always a two-way anguish (whatever the ratio, whatever the provocation or explanation or qualification), maybe vigorous attention to this theorem will help you to become a healing influence in some parent's pain.

Ready?

Willing?

All right, let's think together for a little while about this theorem.

First, as general background, we would need to affirm that a great deal of happiness and nurtured trust and appreciation does exist among American young people and their parents. In fact, without so much glad loyalty all around, the hurts wouldn't ache so dreadfully when they occur. (Paradox upon paradox.) After the latest Thanksgiving vacation on our campus, I suggested to my sophomores, about fifty of them, that each one mention a very specific gratitude as we started class. I was interested to notice the high fraction of those who said "my family" or "my parents" or "my wonderful family" or "my folks," in naming primary gratitudes. Yes, good relationships do exist.

Yet, back to our theorem: so much of pain. So much of tension, anger, resentment, stark anguish. After some thousands of conversations during the past dozen years, I'm convinced of the *much*. After all I have read and observed, noticed and pondered about. Sometimes the emotional cost of getting from childhood to maturity may be very great—indeed, far greater than we usually admit to.

Within evangelical Christian homes there may be a particular unwillingness to acknowledge unresolved tensions. "We're *Christians*," says the implicit reasoning process. "*Christians* love each other and get along beautifully with each other. So we get along fine. So shut up, Junior, and do your chores the way I told you to, and, no, of course you can't have the car tonight. . . . "

And to be angry with a father or hurt by a father is not exactly like any other human pain. In deep, subliminal ways we want to honor a father, admire him, respect him, be praised and valued by him. Since Sinai our innermost selves know that there ought to be harmony between us, and a sickness of spirit infects us while it is absent.

The prevalence of pain.

Some time ago I was emotionally jolted when I handled, within a few days' time, three different short stories from student writers: each story was brilliant, powerful, and dire—and each centered on a son's anger toward a father. Each was a segment of human life transmuted to art and recorded with burning intensity. Each gave me a new window on youthful trauma.

Still feeling the intensity of those three narratives, I mentioned them to a wise and discerning colleague of mine. Not surprising, he nodded, when father-son tensions are so very common in our society.

The prevalence of pain.

A different sort of jolt went through me when I was chatting with a man—call him Marvin Jones—whose distinguished father I had met and respected. When I told Marvin about a delightful theme his sister had written lauding Dr. Jones as a father, he answered in such a grim and quiet way that all my happy excitement went skittering. Marvin still seemed to grit his teeth in remembering Dr. Jones' demeanor to him. Dr. Jones was wise and honored, but his legacy to Marvin was a legacy of pain.

Another jolt when my student Lennie told me a little about his background, and the fierce antipathies that sometimes made him leave the dining table to vomit when his father was at home. (I wonder what the flames of Lennie's emotions are incinerating now. Where are you, Lennie? Emotionally, vocationally, where are you? As a spirit-pilgrim, where are you?)

A different kind of jolt when parents are the receivers of pain rather than the givers. At a national meeting I greeted one of the leaders and spoke of his son, my former student, who was also at the meeting. Mr. Leader's face seemed to turn pavement-gray, and his voice became like a Sir Laurence Olivier doing King Lear. "We have had our hearts broken this week," he said. Broken. Broken. I'm not sure I have ever heard eight sadder words, on stage or off.

A close parallel, though, when a woman I know talked with me a little about her tumultuous young-adult grandchildren and her son, their father. "David has had his heart *broken*," she told me with immeasurable pity and grief. (Immeasurable, inconsolable. The ache of it still aches inside my ears.)

Do I sound too dark, too pessimistic?

I am well aware, believe me, that Scripture admonishes us to think on the things that are pure, lovely, true, virtuous, and "of good report." I am by inclination and habit an optimist, and I always tend to go about sharing bright pieces of new news with acquaintances. Yet for growth and healings to happen we all need to recognize symptoms when they are present. We all need to hear groans when groans are being voiced.

The prevalence of pain.

If you are one of the pain-persons right now, do you feel pushed toward screaming agony sometimes because the ache-free people so ignore your misery? Does it happen especially in churches? You hear preachers laud the family as the bulwark of America, or express gratitude for their own fine sons, and you feel like bashing someone with your fists? Courage to you; Grace, and patience.

If you are a pain-person, you may wince or sneer or laugh outright, quite justifiably, when you look through the greeting card racks and the little books of sentimentality that some publishers like to offer. I saw such a volume a few weeks ago and restrained myself from laughing raucously right there in the bookstore. I did purchase a copy to howl against in more private circumstances. Schmaltzy photos and kitsch drawings accentuate the unthinking sentimentality of its pages. Its composite assertion is that every man who produces a child immediately becomes totally wise, totally gentle, totally affectionate; that every child is totally appreciative, totally devoted, totally loyal toward his sire.

Probably the canny editors of that sentimentality will sell far more copies of such thoughts than if it were entitled *Filial Misery* or *The Pain of Parenting*—or even, like Chad Walsh's fine anthology of poems about marriage, *The Honey and the Gall*. Conceivably, a neutral title, *To Father*, (like unto the title it actually wears) could stand upon the cover of a realistic volume that would be honest enough to writhe and beat its fists as well as burbling in happy peace.

Pain is.

Filial pain is.

No matter how much you hurt, will it be an astringent lotion to you to realize that you are not the only one who knows your kind of pain?

And there are other lotions I'd like you to think about. One: To help someone else in his anguish will strengthen you for your own. It's a principle written deep into human nature. Try it, try it, try it! Somewhere near you are other hurting persons.

Another: New relationships can come to you to supplement what has been in the past, to soften and smooth abrasive memory-edges.

An example? All right. My scholarly friend George, who has done brilliant studies of C. S. Lewis and got to know Lewis as a personal friend. In his teens George had known numbing pain and anger at home. He hasn't said so in print, to my knowledge, but it's my sturdy conjecture that George found in Lewis both a borrowed father and veritable therapy for all the old scars. Maybe he initially and unknowingly reached out to Lewis because he was needing just such therapy.

And another beyond all others and yet melded with them: Whatever one's kind of grief and wretchedness and sickness of the spirit, God's grace is available as antidote and medication. Just last Sunday I heard a resonant sermon inviting our attention to Psalm 46, and my spirit fairly clapped its hands and did cartwheels all through the sermon. In every human predicament to which we admit him, God is refuge, God is strength. In the prevalence of filial pain, most certainly, God is refuge, God is strength.

4

ONLY ONE VERB

Good morning.

It's early morning in Illinois. Maybe it's 3:00 A.M. in New York City as you turn these pages. Maybe it's midnight in San Francisco, or afternoon coffee break time in an office in Idaho, or twilight at a lake in Minnesota.

I look over at just-past-dawn sunlight filtering through an east window, turning leaves on a tall poinsettia to bright stained glass, and I yearn for the intensity of a Mark Antony shouting to the populace in ancient Rome: "Friends, Romans, countrymen, lend me your ears." In New York or San Francisco or Idaho or anywhere else on our whirling big blue marble of a planet, will you "lend me your ears"? I want to talk for a little while about a distinction I believe to be exceedingly important. Oh, exceedingly.

I want to make a distinction you may think, at first, to contain several plain and fancy kinds of hair-splitting, but stay with me. Please?

Did you notice that the sixth command that thundered down from the Sinai slopes contains only one verb? You are to *honor* your father and your mother. It's a terse, explicit, and exclusive kind of imperative. What the ancient Israelis heard thunders to us still in one verb, thunders to every high school kid in America, thunders across the college campuses, too, and into offices where young business people in their twenties and thirties are currently employed, thunders to housewives in suburbia: *Honor* your father and your mother.

Immediately one thinks of the contrast with Brother Paul's admonition in Ephesians 6:1. There, before he quotes the Sinai word, he issues a different command: we are to *obey* our parents—with a qualifier, "in the Lord," and a reassurance, "for this is right." If I understand rightly, Brother Paul is not addressing the housewives in suburbia nor those young business people in their twenties and thirties. His instruction is not, "Hey, you adults, if your parents are still living, you are to *obey* them." Granted, some senior citizens like to read that translation between the lines. (Do you know a tyrant of 79 or 83 or 92 who still whips out commands as though Junior were still ten or eleven years old?)

No, Paul is saying that children, while they are children, are to obey.

And precisely there, of course, comes the friction point in millions of homes as young people move into their teens. "Moth-er!" screams Susie. "You treat me like a child! I'm not a baby any more!" But she isn't an adult, either. "Of course you can't, Johnnie!" says Father in curt vexation. "You're my child, and we don't. . . ." But John-nie is not now a child, not any longer. Still a son, but not a child-son.

To honor, then, and to obey are not synonyms. Certainly they are related, and through the teen years they will often be like two in-separable layers of epidermis.

But honor is—honor. One verb only. "A rose is a rose is a rose," said quixotic genius Gertrude Stein. To honor is to honor is to honor.

And a crucial thing to notice (to experiment with, to live out in the emotional intensities of day by day by day) is that *honor* is a voli-tional verb. You *choose* to honor a person you are speaking with, by the tones of your voice and the things you say, or you choose to dishonor him. You *choose* actions, attitudes, responses.

In contrast, some of the other verbs in a family relationship are simply beyond our choosing, and I think we should frankly recognize that fact. Otherwise needless and wrong guilt feelings will ac-cumulate.

Through the painful events of a lifetime, *trust* may be a verb that no longer works between you and your father. If he has broken his promises and broken his promises and broken his promises, you can-not any longer choose whether you will trust him or not. The trust is gone, evaporated away like rain evaporating from desert sand dunes.

If you are like Kent, disillusioned by your father's extramarital af-fairs and divorce and dismal new marriage, *respect* is not a verb you can choose to enact. Some shreds of "I respect" may still be there when you think of his public speaking ability or his handsome profile or his success in business, but you don't choose whether to respect or not; those choices are made for you by what he is and by what you are.

Maybe "to like" is another verb that is now beyond your choos-ing. As I mention that possibility, my mind slides back to my childhood, to a time when my parents went to call on a neighbor whose husband had just left her and their many children. The fiction writer in me wishes I could do a rerun now on that whole scene; there was more emotional dynamite present than child-me realized. I remember that Mrs. Blank never spoke her husband's name and never let herself say "my husband." Every reference was to "the children's father"; that term for him caught the curious ear of child-me. I remember that she talked a little about how he had beaten her with a rope. I think she invited my mother to have a look at the still-visible bruises on her body, and that my mother gently declined. Looking back, I doubt whether Mary or Betty or George or Katie Blank could have honestly said "I like him." Maybe, though, he was debonair enough when he was not flailing someone with a rope so that some of them did like him in some measure. But "I like" or "I don't like," at deep and honest levels of that verb's use, is something given, not something chosen.

(Granted, preferences change. If you become a different human being, you may like some things you do not now prefer. But we are talking about right now and what your father is like right now.)

Have you read C. S. Lewis's autobiography, *Surprised by Joy*? If you have, you will remember that with careful honesty he tells about his father's eccentric temperament and utterly illogical mind, about the strains he lived with in being his father's son. In all candor, "I like him" is not a phrase young Lewis could always have chosen to use about his father.

Some time ago I saw a very poignant interview on television. A young man—call him Richard—was being asked for comment after the reporters had reviewed the story of his family. His father had habitually beaten Richard's mother and the children and choked them and brutally, savagely tormented them. Once Richard had even experienced a skull fracture from a paternal battering. Finally his despairing mother had hired a killer. Now Richard's father was in a cemetery and his mother in a prison.

The interviewer probed about Richard's feelings for that father, and his face was hauntingly intense, like a very Hamlet's, while he answered. "I loved him," Richard said with tormented earnestness. "No, I didn't *like* him. I didn't like what he did to us. But he was my father. He gave me life. Yes, I loved him."

To "like" had been taken beyond Richard's choosing. In less brutal ways, but as finally and as painfully, maybe "to like" has been moved out of your present possibility, too. If it has, you will need to be realistic and go on from here.

If you are totally honest, you may be wincing as you hear Richard's story, for you aren't at all sure that "I love" is open to you now. Tangled love, maybe? Love mixed with resentment and hate, maybe? Perhaps we should come back to the topic of mixed emotions on another day and think more about it. For now, as the sunlight moves down and down on poinsettia leaves, let's come back to the Sinai verb. It resonates through all of human history, and it summons us: To honor.

"How can I?" you protest. "How can I pretend to honor what isn't honorable? Just tell me that! And he isn't, he isn't, he isn't. . . ."

I look at the complex veining on the back of a leaf, highlighted now by the newest sunbeam, and I think of God's sunlight on the complex underside of everything that is. Sometimes the honor you give will go out to your father because you are honorable and not because he is. Can you carve that principle into the inner surfaces of your soul? The gentle man does gentle deeds. The courageous man does deeds of courage. The faithful man does deeds of faith. And the honorable man does deeds of honor.

An analogy, of a sort. If a state fair announces a prize for the ten thousandth person to enter the turnstiles, the prize will be awarded to the comer when he comes because he is Number 10,000, and not because he is tall or short, kind or cruel, courteous or a cad, handsome or hideous to look upon. The state fair PR people will be gratified if he turns out to be an utterly splendid mortal, but his award will be because of his specified identity, not because of his qualities.

Is that like your circumstances? To honor is your commission, your opportunity, your command—not because of what he is, but because of who he is. And because of who you are—an honorable son who is willing to accept the commission, to follow through on the opportunity, to meet the command.

Someone grits his teeth, and a growl lurches around inside his handsome throat. "How?" he mutters. "What do you want me to *do*?"

Start thinking, friend, and let's come back to that on another day. Okay? Could you make it the business of your life for the next six months, say, to think through what indeed it will mean for you to honor him?

I'll offer some explicit suggestions before we finish talking things through, I promise you, but please don't just wait for them nor stop with them! Interview some people you know and love and trust. Ask them how you can honor him. Experiment and experiment and experiment. Maybe you will like to get a spiral notebook and keep a record of the experiments, or at least of some of them.

And will you talk with Jehovah God about what he meant, and means, by that one verb in your own life?

5

HIS SON, NOT HIS PUPPET

On your block, in your town, in this present year Anno Domini, what does it mean to honor a father? What does it not mean?

Among all the tentative ponderings any of us could offer, one axiom seems to deserve being carved in stone or hammered in bronze: *You are to be his son, not his puppet.*

When you were a child he commanded and you obeyed—I hope. Otherwise, you have even more debris to clear away and even more new foundations yet to pour as you build your house of life. Maybe you had your times of struggle from the era child psychologists call "the terrible twos" onward. Yet you were a child, and a child's province is to be instructed, informed, commanded—to obey. Through it all, however, you were a new identity, a *you*, and not merely a father's toy. Not a father's puppet, even then. As you move on and on into maturity, the axiom becomes more clearly visible in tall stone letters: his son, not his puppet.

Have you ever been backstage in a puppet show? Have you watched skillful fingers lift, turn, manipulate, and maneuver the controls? Slight motion, responsive strings, and the puppet walks, bows, dances, gesticulates. Bobbing motions dip forward and backward. The puppet master flicks a thumb, shifts an arm, and the puppet kneels, curtsies, bows off stage, returns. The puppet master speaks in a shrill falsetto, and the doll figure seems to be declaiming or conversing.

For an evening's amusement a puppet show may be pleasant enough. In real life puppetry can be dismay and sheer anguish.

You think I'm exaggerating? That it doesn't really happen? I wish that were the case. But whether it's fully carried through or not, it's attempted all too often.

The X family, for example. Duane X has finished a graduate degree, and his father has been twitching hard on all the control strings he can touch. "You will settle here in Texas for good, won't you? There's an opening—I told Mr. Wheatley about you—There's a house down the street; we'll help with the down payment—" But Duane has an offer he values from a good firm in Buffalo (or Seattle, or Duluth, or Kankakee). The challenge is right, his sense of providential leading is almost like an Abraham's, he's confident it is his present opportunity.

"I'm going," he says.

Dad X is incredulous, dismal, angry, dismayed. A puppet has no right to kick off the control cords and walk off the stage! Mom X adds her tears. Dad X refuses to help Duane and his wife load the U-Haul.

The Y family.

Tom Y is getting bitter denunciations also, let's say, because he has decided to teach physical education. "But we've counted on you to take over the store," his father grumbles angrily. "I can't keep going forever, Tom. That hardware has been in the Y family for a hundred years! It's a legend through fifteen counties! You know that."

"But I'm not a hardware man, Dad," says Tom. "No way."

"You can become one. I had other ideas, too, when I was a young whippersnapper, but your granddad pulled me into line. . . ."

Pulled puppet strings. And puppet became puppet master.

The Z family. Is there a Z family in every town in America—and on a good many farms?

Jack is the junior partner now, working with John in the Z and Z Construction Company. But "partner" is a misnomer. Jack does the errands that John assigns. Jack agrees with the decisions John has already made. Jack comes and goes and speaks and turns when John twitches the puppet strings. "Yes, Dad. Yes, Dad. I understand. Of course, Dad." His puppet, not his son.

Mr. X and Mr. Y and Mr. Z are fictional men, yet they are not totally fictional, for their prototypes do inhabit the land. In fact, a man who is constantly counseling young adults in his denomination from coast to coast talked to me intensely only days ago about the young people like Duane X and Tom Y and Jack Z whom he sees all too often.

The right goal of parenting, surely, is to bring young people to a responsible maturity in which they make right choices—and make them independently, untwitched by any puppet strings. The very highest honor you can give your father, then, may be to make the right and valid choice when choices are obscure and difficult—even if what you opt for is the stark opposite of what he would command you toward.

Now obviously one seldom knows fully in the instant of decision-making whether he has blundered or fumbled or caused the very angels to rejoice with him. Yet we do not escape the fact that life on planet earth is an intricate maze of decision after decision after decision, nor the further fact that maturity means responsibility in the decision-making process.

The person who has indeed been brought up in the way he should go chooses the high trail, the difficult goal, the faithful task, the altruistic endeavor, the course of valor. In so choosing, he does honor to the persons who have helped to shape his ideals and train his very identity.

Some of the choices will be life-huge. (A vocation. Where one works at the vocation. Whether one marries. Whom one marries. When one marries.) Some decisions will seem miniscule—although a look back from far shores of Forever may see that some of the tiny ones were hinges for very big doors.

In every choice character is being revealed; in every choice one's paternity is being saluted or dishonored.

I write these paragraphs on a Saturday evening in winter. In your town what would a random census show young men to be doing from 9:00 until midnight tonight? What would you guess? Reading comics, reading Plato, reading novels? Smoking pot? Drinking beer at a singles bar? Playing basketball? Preparing a sermon? Spending time with cheap women and cheap booze in a university's darker corners?

Each man chooses, chooses, chooses the way his soul will go. As he chooses, he honors or does not honor his father. When he chooses nobly, he honors his family much more than he would if he were a twitching puppet.

Okay so far, you say. I'm not supposed to let him think and decide for me; I'm not to be a puppet. I'm to honor him by making independent decisions and making them wisely. Sounds good.

But how does one unfasten the puppet strings?

If you're a junior in college and Dad hasn't ever let you make one significant decision. . . . If you're twenty-six years old and he still expects you to come and go at his pleasure. . . . If you're seventeen and he wants to twitch his little finger and designate your college, your major, your vocation, your summer job, your prospective roommate, your girl friend. . . . How *does* one unfasten the puppet strings?

Not easily.

I smile a little and think ruefully that what St. Paul told the Philippians in another context has its applicability: You must "work out your own salvation with fear and trembling." Might these thoughts have their usefulness?

. . . Sometimes, could you mention to Dad a decision that will be coming up and ask him to help you think about the alternatives? Keep the focus, though, on "I must decide." For instance: "Dad, Mr. Jones wants to know whether I'm going on the Glee Club trip during spring break, and I've got to make a decision right away. If I go, I'll lose quite a few hours of work down at Kroger's, but I'll get to see Niagara and

Toronto. Any suggestions before I make up my mind?"

After such a prelude, you'll have to be braced for his anger if your decision doesn't coincide with his recommendations, but you can start establishing a pattern of independent thought and decision.

. . . Sometimes, can you be careful to affirm your loyalty and affection to him (maybe in little and indirect ways) when your actions must challenge his wishes? You go on the glee club tour after he advised against it—*and* you send him a whole series of affectionate postcards. You sign up for guitar lessons, which he scorns as a waste of time—*and* you tuck a book of his favorite cartoons under his pillow. You enroll in the college major he argued against—*and* you send him a telegram of good wishes for his golf tournament.

. . . Sometimes, would it be ultimately beneficial (though very traumatic while it happens) to let Dad know candidly when his string-twitchings pull you toward brinks of desperation? Mortal that he is, he cannot be a mind reader, and he may be quite unaware of the angers he is foisting upon you, of the stuntings he is bringing to your inner self. Can you bring yourself to speak a quiet word upon occasion? "Dad, I think you should know it really tears me up for you to try to plan my whole vacation for me. I don't like ever to be as angry as I was for a while last night. . . . "

. . . Sometimes, would the explaining of your feelings and your needs for growth be more effective in a written note? Maybe the note could be a door-opener for a conversation to follow it.

. . . As you review your present self, and your yesterday self, and the self of all your other yesterdays, might it be good for you to invite some diplomatic outsider to join you and your father for a conversation about your father-son relationship and its tensions? Would the unfastening of the puppet strings happen more easily and more permanently if your pastor or your coach or some other associate could talk with both of you in depth? Maybe a first conversation the friend would have alone with Dad could be usefully informative and eye-opening.

Again, you may need to be braced for paternal anger as an initial response. And the tighter Dad's hands have been holding to the puppet strings, the more incredulous and fierce may be his words to you and your intermediary. (But eventual outcomes may be benedictory.)

. . . Sometimes, can you soften the pain of what seems to be rebellion against him while you tear at those puppet strings by pointedly acknowledging what you have gained from his experience, his perspective, his wisdom, his concern? ("Thanks for the lesson in car-buying today, Dad; when I buy future models and don't have you around to advise me, I'll really remember this." "Prof. Smith was really

impressed, Dad, when I told the Econ. class what you have been saying about our city taxes." "Well, I may go to law school and I may not,
but I'll really keep your pointers in mind while I think about it.
Thanks, Dad.")

. . . Sometimes, often, can your daily devotions include specific
requests for God's own hand upon your growing maturities, upon the
whole of your relationship with your father?

He has a deep investment of affection and concern in you. Your
performance on the transitory stages of this life will always be of utmost interest to him. But for this ultimate enjoyment of your roles as
well as for your skill in the roles you need to be a real-life speaking actor
and not a puppet twitched by little strings.

6

TO COVET A FATHER

Does the demon of covetousness sometimes flap his ugly wide wings and perch on your rooftop, your car aerial, your wincing shoulders? When he singles you out, maybe he keeps you busy coveting cars and stereos and ten-speed bicycles and grades and girl friends. Sometimes, among some mortals, he gets out a particularly nasty weapon from his ugly arsenal: father-coveting. If you're on his prowl list for attack with that weapon, it's time to be pulling on the chain-mail garments.

Has he already pinked you, time and again?

Did you kick trees and fences sometimes when you came home from fifth grade, and mutter inside yourself, "I wish Bobby's father were *my* father?"

Did you play sad games at junior high school events in looking for just the father you would most desire to claim as your own?

Were Parents' Day events sometimes a barbed and spiny wretchedness for you in college because old demon Covet was at your elbow while you watched other families talking and laughing together? You couldn't know all of his obscene tricks, of course. Maybe he was having malevolent glee in prodding half a dozen other fellows to covet *your* father even while you were weaving small edges of a wistful fantasy: "Now if only that genially gracious man over there were *my* father. . . . He looks so intelligent and kind and earnest and good. . . ."

Even with all our computers it isn't possible to do any comprehensive census of the momentary covetous thoughts that can dart through human heads. My strong conjecture, though, is that foul Mr. Covetousness is much busier and more often triumphant than we would ever like to admit. And his weapons are often envenomed like the tip of the sword Laertes used against Hamlet.

Shall I illustrate?

Once years ago I was weekending in a gracious country estate. My host was a choral conductor, my hostess a multilingual and widely traveled scholar. During one of my unwary moments, Covetousness hurled a dextrous javelin at me, and it stung fiercely where it grazed the skin. "If only *I* could have been born into a home like this one," he caused me to murmur inwardly. "Languages, scholarship, foreign travel, the world of great music. Privileges. If these people had been my parents, what might I be by now?"

Almost in an instant common sense provided a shield and Grace handed me some poultices. "Silly girl," I could tell myself. "If you had been born here, you wouldn't be *you*. You'd be someone else, and that someone might actually dislike all that you admire here! Yours was the heritage that made you become *you*!"

And be off with you, Demon Covetousness. Take along your obnoxious assistant, Mr. Self-Pity.

He's tough and resolute, though, that one. He tried another attack once not too many months ago. I was reading a current journal and found an essay in which a slightly pompous writer was expressing gratitude for his whole family heritage, naming off honored positions in evangelical leadership held by his father, his grandfathers, his uncles, his great-uncles. Rather than rejoicing with him as much as I might have, I found myself grumbling ("O you utter snob!") and coveting ("Now if his editor-preacher-writer father had been *my* father . . .").

And again I had to admonish myself, like Shakespeare's King Lear: "O, that way madness lies; let me shun that; no more of that."

Even a touch of coveting can produce unpleasant scars and grim debris if we give way to this demon. We join company with "have-nots" of other kinds and types throughout wide earth who become embittered in watching the "haves." To covet another's wealth, his wife, his house, his job, his anything will leave a sticky black residue upon the soul. To covet a father? No. You must not let it happen. Drive off the demon, like Christian in *Pilgrim's Progress* doing battle with Apollyon, and go on from here.

You have an arsenal of weapons, too. The deft sword of Acceptance is a weapon old Covet cannot face. Have at him, in God's name.

Turn the sword before you put it back into the scabbard. Gently, gently. Left to right. The gleams that dartle from it are worth noticing: gleams of vicarious gladness, as you enjoy another's circumstance with him freely and candidly. Acceptance does its task, and Covet leaves the field.

Now look again. Script is engraved along the blade of this sword. Tall letters in a calligraphy that looks like Greek printing. A motto: "What is that to thee? Follow thou me."

Enjoy other fathers? Yes. Covet other fathers? No. It must not be.

7

I WISH HE WOULDN'T

Suppose.

Suppose a talking-things-through kind of conference were being held on our campus this week here at Greenville College. Suppose you and several hundred other people turned up hoping that somehow, somehow, somehow you would get your inner batteries recharged or your inner wounds healed here, that life will make more sense when you climb back into your Valiant or your VW or your Porsche or your Mustang at the end of the week, when you walk up the loading ramp into an Ozark airplane or TWA or United.

Suppose that this morning, this bitter-bright winter morning, some sixty or seventy of us are in the big lecture room in Snyder Hall for an early session of the conference. Some of you are sipping coffee from styrofoam Snack Bar cups. Some of you are sprawled almost comfortably in the sturdy lecture-room chairs. Some of you, more nearly comfortable, are sitting on the thick orange-brown tweed rug, leaning back against the next tier of the amphitheater floor.

Each of you will have a chance to talk in depth with me sometime later this week or with other people on the conference staff. (Maybe your pastor came with you and is one of the leaders; maybe half a dozen good psychologists are here.)

Okay?

Now suppose I give you an exercise. I pass out blue books like the ones colleges use often for in-class themes and ask you to write for twenty minutes or so, jotting down rapidly whatever comes to your mind after I announce a topic. You don't need to write in full sentences, nor even make sense. Just spill onto the paper whatever drifts through your head. Okay?

Okay.

I pick up a piece of chalk and turn to the smooth brown chalkboard. In big clear script I write the topic: "I WISH MY FATHER WOULDN'T . . . " After writing it, I sit down in a corner of the lecture room and review my notes for my next talk. First, though, I breathe a very earnest prayer: that you will be honest and thorough and utterly candid.

After about seventeen minutes I glance around the room again. Half a dozen fellows are still writing as rapidly as pens can be pushed. Two or three are breaking styrofoam cups into tiny, tiny pieces and looking angry enough to break more than cups. Several seem to be doodling and thinking so hard I hesitate to clear my throat. Up in the back row someone has turned his chair toward the window and is studying Scott Field with such intensity one would think him an artist preparing to paint it from memory.

Okay. "Back to committee of the whole," I invite with a small grin. Now, what you have written is as confidential as you want it to be, I assure everyone. Keep it totally for your own use if you like, or keep it to talk through with a conference leader this week if you like. Are there some of you who would be willing to mention some items you have jotted down? It might help all of us to get a handle on some principles. . . .

Slow restlessness. Hesitation. Then a high school kid on the floor at my left waves his hand, and the back row offers two or three items, and a green letter jacket from Michigan lifts its sleeve. I turn to scribble some words on the chalkboard, and jot down others on my note pad. Some voices are tight with emotion. Some are casually amused, almost nonchalant. Almost. Some rasp and snarl.

I suggest principles that seem to be emerging; you suggest principles to each other.

After a while I glance at the little Timex on my left wrist, confirm its report by a glance up at the wall clock, and quickly pull things to an end before I send you off to the gym for your next session.

What have we heard? Samplings of samplings:

. . . I wish he wouldn't leave his boots in the living room and clomp around the house in his socks when he comes home from work.

. . . I wish he wouldn't yell at me so much about my grades.

. . . I wish he wouldn't call me "Ralphie," as though I were still two years old.

. . . I wish he wouldn't try to make my business decisions for me; I'm thirty-two years old, but he thinks I'm still twelve.

. . . I wish he wouldn't fight with Mom so often.

. . . I wish he wouldn't bug me so much about mowing the yard and washing the car and everything.

. . . I wish he wouldn't boom at his friends halfway across the room when I'm at a restaurant with him.

. . . I wish he wouldn't talk so much about me to visitors when I'm right there, as though I were his champion steer on display at the County Fair! He acts as though I don't have a tongue in my own head.

. . . I wish he wouldn't say "You kin betcher bottom dollar" fifteen hundred times a day.

. . . I wish he wouldn't disappear into the boob tube and his beer cans right after supper every night of the world.

. . . I wish he wouldn't tease me so cotton-pickin' much about any girl I ever talk with for two minutes.

. . . I wish he wouldn't just assume that I'm going to be his law partner some day. I'm not, I'm not, I'm not, I'm not.

. . . I wish he wouldn't pick his teeth in public.

. . . I wish he wouldn't ridicule me so much when I'm driving.

. . . I wish he wouldn't play favorites. My older brother can't do anything wrong in his eyes; I can't do anything right.

. . . I wish he wouldn't push me toward sports so much. I'd rather be playing the piano or my guitar or a jew's-harp!

. . . I wish he weren't so insanely intense in his political ideas.

. . . I wish he wouldn't wear his crummy old hunting caps when he goes downtown.

. . . I wish he wouldn't leave drawers and cupboard doors standing open after he looks for something.

. . . I wish he wouldn't treat my wife like a silly Shirley Temple doll.

. . . I wish he wouldn't go on such humongous long business trips and care so little about anything but business when he gets back. Last year I was the starting pitcher at the JuCo and he didn't see one home game; other guys had their dads yelling for 'em at half of the away games or more.

. . . I wish he wouldn't barge into my apartment without knocking.

. . . I wish he wouldn't say "ain't" and talk about "goin'" and "doin'" and "comin'"; I wish he wouldn't tell me to "pass them beans."

. . . I wish he wouldn't tell his same jokes fifty thousand times a year.

. . . I wish he wouldn't quiz us and scold us about what my wife spends on her clothes.

. . . I wish he wouldn't assume that I believe exactly what he believes about everything, and freeze up if I even ask him to explain something he does believe.

. . . I wish he wouldn't grumble so much about the kind of car I chose to buy.

. . . I wish he wouldn't be so flirty with waitresses. He would say he's just being happy and sociable, but Mom hates it. And so do I.

. . . I wish he wouldn't pick on me so much about my posture. Just because he was in the Marines. . . .

. . . I wish he wouldn't always squeeze the toothpaste from the middle of the tube.

. . . I wish he wouldn't act so suspicious around my friends. He pesters them as though he were a prosecuting attorney, or maybe a detective.

* * *

You leave Snyder Hall, all of you, and go on up to the gymnasium. I erase the chalkboards, gather my scribbled notes, tap the blue books into a smoother pile to take up to my office for browsing in before I return them to you, before you talk with the counselors about what you have written there—if talking is your choice, and I hope it will be.

Back at my desk, I jot down notes about some of the principles that were starting to emerge in our discussion, some we'll want to probe more deeply. Some that aren't obviously apparent, but are pretty important.

First of all, is it utterly evident that the strains and tensions of "I wish he wouldn't . . . " are very, very prevalent among human sons?

I hope you aren't carrying around undue baggage of guilt feelings because you feel some tensions. People do feel them. Christian people do feel them. Different tensions should be faced and understood and worked through, not evaded and ignored. Sometimes church and family traditions have been grievously at fault in causing us to think that obedience, respect, and admiration are the only feelings a decent fellow can possibly have toward his father. Well, they aren't. Honorable, upright Christian fathers may still cause great friction to their sons, even if they are honorable, upright Christian sons. And if any one of those six adjectives I've just spoken gets displaced temporarily or for longer pieces of time, the frictions may produce harsh grinding noises and cause huge pain.

Just hours ago I talked long distance with a wonderfully sensitive young man who is carrying outstanding leadership in his denomination. Before the conversation ended, Jim mentioned a recent holiday visit to his parents and his new realization that he and his father still have "unfinished business" emotionally to work through. A lot of his contemporaries are in the same plight, Jim is realizing, and the plight isn't made easier when the parent generation tends to bridle and say, by implication if not directly, "How *dare* you have those feelings?" Jim was deeply affected, he now understands, by the Vietnam era; his father was just as deeply affected by other eras. Each needs to reach out to the other at deeper and deeper levels. Jim's rapidly flexible tones of voice let me know that he is trying to reach, and to reach.

And so are you, who wrote in these blue books.

First, then, *the principle of prevalence.*

Next, it seems to me there's another principle we might call *the pain of proximity.* Some things in your father's lifestyle bother you because he is so close to you, so much a part of you. Little traits, little habits, little eccentricities you would merely smile at in someone else's relative can sting like sunburn or throb like migraine when they are the traits of your very own father.

Can you recognize that fact and step back enough to gain objectivity?

If he weren't so dear to you, he wouldn't have so much power to annoy you, dismay you, anger you as he does. The pain of proximity. This principle has come into focus for me repeatedly when I have worked through George Eliot's great novel *Adam Bede* with a class of sophomores. In an early chapter as she introduced her title character and his fretful mother, the author paused to write a small essay.

"Family likeness has often a deep sadness in it," she observed. "Nature, that great tragic dramatist, knits us together by bone and muscle, and divides us by the subtler web of our brains; blends yearning and repulsion; and ties us by our heartstrings to the beings that jar us at every moment. We hear a voice with the very cadence of our own uttering the thoughts we despise; we see eyes—ah! so like our mother's—averted from us in cold alienation; and our last darling child startles us with the air and gestures of the sister we parted from in bitterness long years ago. The father to whom we owe our best heritage—the mechanical instinct, the keen sensibility to harmony, the unconscious skill of the modeling hand—galls us, and puts us to shame by his daily errors; the long-lost mother, whose face we begin to see in the glass as our own wrinkles come, once fretted our young souls with her anxious humors and irrational persistence."

Well, like some other brilliant essays, that Eliot paragraph does not tell the whole truth, but it does contain truth. There can be a pain in proximity, and to identify our pains candidly will help us in coping with them.

Sometimes on some matters could you work toward a lessening of tension if you could just talk about the tension point? Talk quietly, calmly, in a matter-of-fact way. No fireworks. Could you? Maybe Dad has no idea that some of his habits annoy you as violently as they do. Instead of raging inwardly with silent lava burning in your arteries, could you toss out a casual "Hey, Dad, have you ever thought about squeezing the toothpaste tube up from the bottom?"

A small and ancient scar twinges inside me. I had a roommate once who was a splendid person but often a very silent person. I was utterly startled one evening when she barked angry rage at me over a small detail of my housekeeping (or not keeping) habits. "If you don't *quit. . . ,*" she snarled. And I had to wonder why she had never said "Let's . . . " or "Wouldn't it be better to . . . " long before she came to that point of incendiary wrath and scorched the far side of my soul's pale epidermis. Are your silences with Dad too often like her too-long-lasting silences toward me?

The principle, then, of *talking things over.* Can you experiment with it, and experiment with it, and keep on experimenting with it?

Another principle, in the form of a query. Is some of what you resent in your father a resentment that your own nature calls into being? Are there lingerings of what the American frontier would have called your "cussedness"? Is Dad still endeavoring to train you up in some of the ways you should go—as Solomon's Proverbs instructed him to do—and is your carnality resisting all the training?

So he yells at you about your posture. Well, would you be more handsome to everyone else, too, if your spine didn't sag so much? So he is constantly "on your case" about your grades? Well, what must you report, when you are honest, about your study habits, your use of the libraries, the use of your mind?

Consider a parable or two from the visual arts. One could imagine that white marble doesn't exactly enjoy being pounded and chipped and hammered and rubbed, but a block of raw stone doesn't become a statue of David nor a *Pietà* without pressure upon it. The mahogany coffee table in my living room didn't grow to be gleaming and polished and lovely in its lines without pain and discipline from saws and sandpaper.

The principle, then? *Some stresses with a parent may be part of the ongoing parenting process by which you can come to a fuller maturity.*

You aren't meant to be counted still an adolescent when you are middle-aged, of course; we'll talk more on another day about the "deparenting" process. But when an anger kicks you violently, should you inquire whether some part of it is anger against a chastisement that you deserve? In this context turn in your Bible to Hebrews 12:11; probably the rich lilt of the KJV is to be preferred here to some of the modern versions: "Now no chastening for the present seemeth to be joyous, but grievous: nevertheless afterward it yieldeth the peaceable fruit of righteousness unto them which are exercised thereby."

Sometimes, "I wish he wouldn't" means you are being "exercised thereby." Does it not?

Sometimes, in another fashion, do you struggle because what he is diminishes or shadows or insults your own self-image? Is there an *ego-protection principle* at work here, too? Whatever other fathers are, you would like your father to be wise and benevolent and handsome and esteemed? Deep inside you cherish a desire to be admired, a feeling that you deserve to be admired. To gain more of the admiration, you would like to have a dream-perfect father, and you resent him when he is ordinary mortality? Is it sometimes so?

Just as Hollywood and the TV scripts have given American husbands and wives vain goals to pursue and think they deserve, our modern folklore has too often fed us with notions of rather ridiculous perfection in all things: shampoo, deodorant, lawn tools, dog food. And we come to feel that we, precious *we*, deserve perfection in our forebears and our associates, too.

So?

So what will I tell you when you come in later this week to talk about what you wrote in the blue book?

This, I think. Sometimes a father needs emotional elbow room, needs the freedom to be himself. Throughout human history, and especially since the 1960s in America, young people have been asserting at various levels of belligerence,"But I've got to be *me*." Yes. Finding your own identity and your own maturity is a great quest. But at the same time he has got to be *he*. And your humor, your resilience, your comprehending patience, your durable gentleness will enable that possibility to happen as it could not otherwise. Your experiments in honoring him are very, very important.

As I continue to sort this great pile of "I wish he wouldn't" statements, one sheaf emerges that needs a different sort of comment. In ultimate implication papers in this sheaf are saying, "I wish he wouldn't run from God; I wish he wouldn't evade his moral responsibilities." (Were thoughts like those in the mind of the young man who studied Scott Field with such fierce intensity while people wrote in blue books in Snyder Hall this morning?)

And we're brought bang up against another principle, one of the deepest-running and most powerful of them all: *God himself is involved in our human plights, our human tensions.*

For this kind of "wish he wouldn't" there is the ultimate resource of intercession. One might feel he's moving over into a kind of selfish cheapness when he bends his knees about personal situations, and prayer could conceivably be mere evasion. But real prayer does not stop with "Please make Dad a Christian so he will be nicer to me." Prayer invites God's full will and hews pathways through twisted jungle vines for his will to walk upon. Prayer builds a highway through the desert, fills up valleys, slices off mountains and hills for construction process. (Yes, I'm looking at Isaiah 40.)

To pray the earnest, durable, persisting prayers that will, in God's grace, bring your father closer to God himself—what greater privilege could there be in this world?

And in fact whether Dad is an utter pagan or a stumbling new Christian or a seasoned and mature churchman, all the possible friction points of "I wish he wouldn't" and "I wish he would" are appropriate topics to bring before your heavenly Father, are they not? God's children cannot have a concern too tiny for his loving care. Remember those two sparrows that were to be sold for a tiny farthing but were not outside the scope of God's awareness, Jesus said (Matthew 10:20). And he said further that the very hairs of your head are all numbered.

If God knows and cares how many thready little filaments stuck in your comb this morning and how many are still anchored to your scalp, you can be sure he knows when you yearn against your human father's newest pagan deeds. When you grit your teeth because of Dad's mannerisms. When you choke on what you feel to be Dad's unfairness to you or his cruelty or his folly.

While I urge you to pray earnestly about your father and the dissonances between you, I am thinking of a useful word about husbands and wives that might be transferred over to meet your situation also. A radiantly winsome woman I talked with in California told me that she was passing on to the Christian wives of not-yet-Christian men this thoughtful counsel: "Remember, it's *your* business to make him happy; it's *God's* business to make him good." I don't know where Winifred had picked that bundle of fragrance, but it was worth the picking. And I hand a sprig of it on to you in your present circumstance: It's *your* business—insofar as you can, and as God helps you—to make your father happy; it's *God's* business to make him good.

And if Dad doesn't ever change one whit in the future, if he keeps all the traits you now feel to be sand in your teeth and smog against your eyeballs?

Well, then—listen carefully—you will have some opportunities, a day at a time, for new experiments with all-inclusive love. It's no big deal, after all, to love what is lovely. But Jesus summoned us to much, much more than reciprocal kindness. "You invite me to dinner and I'll invite you" may be nice, but it's not beyond kindergarten level in Christian discipleship, is it? "You be good to me and I'll be good to you." Kindergarten level. Jesus talked about loving enemies. We have read Matthew 5 so many times that the words slide over our minds without seeping in, don't they? Enemies, enemies, *enemies*! So what about Dad when he leaves his work shoes in the living room or picks his teeth in public or makes snide remarks about the cost of your wife's newest gown? He's to be loved and to be loved and to be loved, that's what.

In imagination I tap my pile of blue books into a firmer pile once more, and then I reach for a notebook of my unpublished poems. What I've just been saying to you reminds me of a shaking-up our Lord Christ gave me once some years ago when I had been writhing inwardly and accumulating some ugly flotsam and jetsam inside of me over a rather dreadful colleague. (Or one I found rather dreadful. There's a difference.) I was living with annoyance. Stress. Disgust. Disgust with myself. Tension. Anger. Tension. "I wish. . . ." And these lines came into being:

> Dear God,
> I cannot stand him; oh, I cannot stand
> that man.
> His ego is a panzer column
> rolling over, over
> everyone.
> He lurches through our lives
> and makes demands
> until we're like woodlands uprooted
> for highway construction
> but he is no highway to anywhere
> except to his own prides.
> Dear God,
> how can I face
> his crashing crushing devastating ways
> for one more day?
>
> * * *
>
> I think the smile of our Lord Christ
> was very sad;
> I think I glimpsed
> oozing new-moist blood along the scars
> on the back of His hands.
>
> I think he says I am to pray about
> some bright and moving flames,
> some new high-voltage currents,
> some generating winds
> that will carry power enough
> to recycle all of us
> including a panzer ego:
> including a me.

No, in all candor I can't say that everything was suddenly sweetness and light and stayed sweetness and light forever and ever between me and The Dreadful One. But I recognized a discernable strength in my then-situation. And to his Strength I would commend you in your now-situation. Yours and that of every blue book in my whole imagined pile and of every not-imagined "blue book" in millions of homes all across America!

8

TO KEEP A SILENCE?

Silence is golden, says the proverb. Often it is, but not always. Sustained silence about one's deep emotional turmoils may be a gracious chivalry in protecting the one who causes the turmoil, and it may be a valiant stoicism in attempting to shoulder one's own troubles. Yet too long and too totally sustained silence may be a diseased sort of self-protecting pride.

When a father is unbearable, is it better to ignore him utterly in all your conversations? Should you address high heaven about him and address unresponding bedposts or floor lamps about him, but otherwise keep sturdy silence? Does the honoring of a father require prevailing silence as a minimum essential?

Certainly you will have a care, in honorable loyalty, about what you say and to whom. Steady silences when dorm neighbors are talking about family trips, family plans, and family memories may be your generous equivalent to the filial respect of old Noah's sons, Shem and Japheth. Remember? When Noah lay drunk and naked in his tent after he became a grower of vineyards, Shem and Japheth took a robe and walking backwards into the tent dropped it on their nude father to hide his shame from staring onlookers.

In our time muckraker journalism and widening disregard for privacy sometimes make us feel wistful for more Shem-people and Japheth-people. Have you read biographies and heard conversations that showed so little reticence about anything that your face felt scorched?

As I ask, I hear a younger version of me in Italy one time saying to a member of my tour group (about as sharply as I have ever said anything to anyone), "Look, I should not be *hearing* what you are telling me! Now let's talk about something else." That fluently gossiping mind had seemed quite unable to censor anything, and dishonor was pouring out in rivulets of sewage.

In utter contrast I think of valiant Dick. I had an occasion to telephone Dick's home once when his parents' divorce was near the final stages. Maybe it had already been granted; I don't recall precisely. I do recall how deftly Dick—then a teen-ager—took my message, gave me news about himself, talked cheerily about his plans, and opened no small crack of a doorway to any discussion of his parents' debacle. He clearly was not about to disclose any smidgen of painful knowledge I might not already have. I was an outsider to their situation, and he adroitly kept me an outsider. Bravo, Dick.

You, too, won't say everything to everyone about your father, no matter how unbearable he is. Not if you live by principles of honor.

Yet your silences could be so total that they will become a veritable pathology.

Shall I mention a story or two?

I had occasions to work rather closely with Ted over quite a period of time. He was my student on an official class roster or two, I bumped into him at a good many campus functions, and I had been in any number of two-person dialogues with him. Ted had never mentioned his father to me. Though I knew vaguely that his was a two-parent home, his observations were always about his mother's plans and expectations for his future. Sometimes I felt a fuzz of annoyance about his lopsided filial loyalty, but I had never asked any pointed questions.

Then, eventually, I met Ted's father, and annoyance dissolved in a swirling mist of pain and dismay. It was a little like meeting Archie Bunker himself. Ted was a student of rare brilliance and decorum; he ate knowledge like fudge and popcorn, he won prizes, he was a walking Mr. Scholarship. In utter contrast his father turned out to be a man of harsh crudities and narrow untrained intellect. And I discerned what Ted had never been able to tell me: he disliked his father so much that he kept silences about him, even with his close associates.

Well, once when I saw Ted later on, he was still not talking about his father, but he did tell me a little about a psychiatrist with whom he had been consulting. I was glad he was getting the professional help he needed, but I wondered and wondered. If he had brought himself to talk at least a little to a few trusted confidants during his earlier years, would the time with a psychiatrist have been less needful for him?

From Ted to Vic and another small narrative—which I'm sure could be a novel as thick as one of James Michener's, if one knew and were to tell Vic's whole biography.

Vic was a friend of mine during one of my getting-educated chapters. A rather close friend. Vic the impetuous; Vic the unpredictable; usually Vic the delightful.

Vic didn't talk much about his family and not at all about his father, if retrospect is accurate. I didn't particularly notice his silences at the time, although I was vaguely curious about Vic's whole antecedent biography when one of my senior professors uttered a cryptic comment about "something" I should perhaps be told about Vic sometime. A good while later a wisp of breeze blew "something" toward me about his father's having been a convict.

We had discussed some ten thousand things while I knew Vic—or maybe 9,736 at a more conservative estimate—but apparently he never let himself dare to talk with me about his unbearable father.

And at the risk of sounding melodramatic I solemnly aver that the latest news I have had about Vic came from a newspaper clipping someone sent me: Vic was in trouble with the law, and a judge was instructing him to get some professional counseling.

And again the haunting need to wonder and wonder. If Vic could have talked through some of his emotions with trusted confidants while they were younger and newer emotions, might the saga of his life have been very different?

Sometimes, yes, silence is golden. Sometimes silence is chivalrous and honoring to another. Sometimes it is a protective epidermis for one's own spirit. But sometimes too much silence is lead or zinc or rusty iron rather than gold. Sometimes silence is pride and folly both at once. Sometimes it is not a mark of wisdom to ignore all of anything in one's daily conversations.

To keep a silence?

Perhaps, and sometimes. May Wisdom guide you well!

9

TO BORROW A FATHER

Good evening, Kent. Hello, George. Welcome, David. Delbert, nice to see you. How are you anyway?

Yes, my imagination is working in lively ways this evening. It is not at all hard to imagine that I've been hearing the doorbell and that a throng of you are here in my home chatting with me about jobs, camping trips, cars. Did you get your VW repaired, Tim? Did the boss come through with your promotion, Jerry?

You laugh at each other, tease each other, mimic each other. Laughter modulates to chuckles and sometimes subsides into long moments of silence before next laughter. In the midst of all your fun there is yearning here, and wistful hunger and anger tangled with resentment, and "I wish" clashing against "I won't."

Orphaned. You're orphaned, all of you. And it's painful to be orphaned, even if yours is the bereavement of emotional distance rather than through any funerals.

Imagination picks up the teapot and hands you a cup. It's Wagner's Fruit and Spice Tea. I hope you like it. Imagination turns down the stereo; the London Philharmonic is getting a little too energetic. Imagination hands you a bowl of carob chips and nuts I've been nibbling from; here, have some.

Before long someone propounds a topic he has really been wanting to discuss:

Whether it's a good thing to go around trying to borrow a father when yours has been mislaid. Is a pinch-hitter of any use at all in this big game?

Well, there's no one quick and single comment anyone could make on that topic. One of my mother's most durable proverbs would certainly apply: "Circumstances alter cases." In general, though, we could quickly hazard an opinion that father-borrowing is often a very healthy and wholesome practice, couldn't we?

What about you, Kent? Any experiences to share with us?

Kent looks thoughtful. "Well, in a way," he hazards, "you could call my boss a father-figure, sort of. He's good to work for—thoughtful—sets high standards for me—praises me pretty lavishly when I come through on a tricky assignment. Yeah, I guess it helps a little in the horrible P.-P.-D. traumas to have *him* over me."

"P.-P.-D.?" We lift collective eyebrows.

"Post-Parental-Divorce," he says grimly.

"Oh. . . . George? Any comments?"

"Um—well—I'm really not much on fraternizing with the elderly, you know, but I spent quite a while talking to one of my chemistry profs on Thursday night. Will that count? It perked me up quite a bit. We talked about a lot of things besides the last chem test."

Duly recorded.

"Mick?"

"Huh? Oh, sorry. I was thinking. Sure. My pastor's great about giving a boost to the old morale. I call him up about twenty times a week. Well, more or less. I hadn't thought of it that way, but, yeah, I guess he is sort of a borrowed father. I didn't see nearly as much of him when Dad was still at home as I do now, that's for sure."

Don seems eager to speak. He hitches forward a little on the camel-leather hassock he's occupying and taps his knees in rhythmic cadence. "Coach Enfield," he says. "My basketball coach, y'know. He yells at me enough to be a real good sub for a father." Don grins. "Hey, I've been thinking. I'll bet one reason so many guys play sports is that they can use a whaddya-call-it—a father figure—in their lives right now. At least half the guys on our first string squad are from Dee-Vorced families. Y'know?"

We know.

The teapot is empty, the stereo records have ended, the carob chips are all gone. Nobody's reaching for his coat yet, though.

My opinion?

Well, all right. You've already been illustrating my opinion. Sometimes you need to be alone and sometimes you need to be with your contemporaries, but sometimes you need interaction with a senior generation. You really do. If your father has opted out of your life or—or—has been pushed out of your life (I'm keeping my eye on the mantel, carefully neutral), then doing things with a surrogate father can be a great idea.

I pause to think for a moment.

Like Tommy, I go on. Tommy called me from his college the other day and talked on and on. He mentioned being entertained at his adviser's home and about going to a football game with one of his other profs. They're not trying to compete with Tommy's absentee father, I gather, but they certainly are supplementing him in getting Tommy more fully civilized.

Now someone is starting to reach for his coat. I ignore him and push ahead, for an idea that seems important has just assailed me.

It could be, I continue, that developing strong rapport with some borrowed fathers will help you, you know, in getting back into sync with your own father. To accept the give-and-take of friendship without the emotional barriers that have built up at home might prepare you for a new level of acceptance across the barriers one of these times.

"You don't think," hazards Don, "that a guy is dishonoring his own father when he borrows a dad sometimes? Like, you're always harping on that big command from Uncle Moses, y'know. . . . "

I know.

But your father's space in your heart is about wide enough for six men to stand in and have room left over, even though you didn't think so when you had your last big hassle with him. Going bowling with a deacon from your church won't fill more than half a crevice in that space, don't worry.

"And maybe the deacon will leave the space a little neater for Dad to step back into?" grins Don. "Hey, I'll buy that."

Now coats are definitely in motion, and gloves. Someone slips into boots he had scuffed off and left over by the front door.

"Oh, must you go? So nice to see you. Good night. Good night. Good night."

You troop out the front door. I latch it behind you, switch off the porch light, and let my mind ramble a little.

Even close-knit homes with a high measure of solidarity need to borrow extra relatives from time to time, I muse. Bishop Dale Cryderman has reminisced in print about how much church friends meant to his wife and him in serving as stand-in parents when the two of them had to be gone together. Almost any family could pay tribute to the extended family. Uncles. Cousins. Grandparents. Neighbors. Boy Scout leaders. Sunday school staff. Coaches. Professors. It happens all the time. But for these guys it's much, much more crucial to find the substitute father, the pinch hitter, the occasional stand-in parent.

I hope they find good ones, not Pied Pipers to lead them into some sleazy, dark nowhere. I'd wish for them someone of the caliber of Dr. Arthur Secord, who taught our university students' Sunday school class when I was in graduate school. He told us once, I recall, that he and Mrs. Secord were buying a larger house for their expanding family, "which of course includes all of you."

To borrow a father can be encouragement and stimulus and solace and reassurance. It can stabilize identity when the turmoils of living have left one's compasses and gyroscopes either out of kilter or mistrusted. It needs common sense, though, lest the borrower lean too hard and place undue demands.

I step over to the front door again and watch the maple trees tossing in the wind along Beaumont Avenue. I think about the many, many times that Bruce paced along Beaumont when he was a student. I wonder how many miles a pedometer would have recorded from his student time as he hiked and biked and hiked across the fields and woods and gentle hills of southern Illinois! Of all I've ever worked with, Bruce was surely one of the most durably angry with a father. Such pain, such pain, such pain. In the campus community there was, fortunately, a man who became important to Bruce, a man he could hear without rebellion and speak to without self-loathings. Now Bruce has gone on to maturities in further study and in employment that I hardly could have hoped for him. To borrow a valuable father was an important part of his maturing, I am sure.

I flick off the living room lamps, settle myself against pillows, pick up a Testament. . . . Help them each, O my Father, to borrow good fathers. . . .

10

TO HONOR IS TO FORGIVE

It's dawn twilight here in Illinois. Thin gray clouds are fleeced across the sky behind still-dark outlines of trees. In my home a fat little yellow candle and a taller wax pillar, flower-scented, brighten drab morning.

I wonder how your morning begins, how it progresses. Are you on a commuter's train from Grand Central Station in New York City right now, reading a morning paper and turning pages abruptly when you catch headlines that grate against unhealed emotions? Are you at an employment office in Ohio filling out forms and gritting your teeth against some of what you must write down? Are you making out a test for a high school history class in California and dawdling over the questions while your mind thumbs again, again, again some of the blotchy ink-spattered pages of your own early American history?

Whatever the outside weather where you are today, how is the weather of your inner self? If I were beside you on the clacking commuter train or in a teachers' lounge, what might you be saying quietly about the climate inside?

Maybe there as here I would have a finger on red-printed columns in a leather-bound volume. Listen to this, I might be telling you. You've heard it and recited it ten thousand times, but listen to it. " . . . And forgive us our trespasses, as we forgive those who trespass. . . . " Our debts; our trespasses; our sins. As we forgive, please forgive us.

Have you thought—recently, strenuously, deeply—about the fact that a primary part of *honoring* a father, at some times in your life, may be forgiving him? Other components of honor coincide with the forgiving or may follow along after the forgiving, but they won't replace it.

Probably no one totally understands the process called forgiveness. As with some of the processes in the scientific world—electricity, magnetism, laser beams, vaccinations—we can know it *is* and value what happens through it without utter comprehension.

Love, retroactively applied. That's the essence of it, surely.

Only you and God can know what you need to forgive when

you think about your father. You can't limit the forgiving to episodes or attitudes for which he explicitly asks your forgiveness, I'm sure of that. He may still view as parental duty some paddlings or decisions that you, receiving, felt to be cruelties against you. He may not have known at all that he was bruising your ego that time at breakfast—that night after the basketball game—that morning when you left for college.

Let realism speak further. Like the ancient Israelis he may be a "stiff-necked and stubborn" person who cannot yet frame the words of an apology or a "please forgive." Could not if the archangels themselves stood visible and commanding at his two elbows.

Yet if your forgiving waits to hear his asking, you will be left with little evil beasts kenneling inside your soul. Better the cleansing.

Are you cocking an eyebrow over those history quizzes, over the newspaper on the commuter train, and muttering "But how *can* I? You don't just suddenly will to forgive somebody and, zap, it's done like a magician's handkerchief trick. . . . "

No, not like that. It's process and miracle and obedience. It's not something you dream up or work out through your own skill and ingenuity. Rather, it is opening yourself to Grace and letting Grace—which is always there and available—flow through you. Lord Alfred Tennyson once said, his son reported, that to him prayer was like opening great sluice gates and letting the sea of God's love pour through. In homelier metaphor, you don't concoct the water in your kitchen plumbing, but you can open a faucet to make water available. You can choose to forgive or refuse to forgive.

I have mentioned elsewhere (in magazine articles and in my book *Free to Be Single*) an experience that once gave me huge new comprehensions of forgiveness; shall I share it with you also?

One summer I reeled under horrible anguish when a brilliant former student of mine was murdered. He was my counselee, my protégé, a close and valued personal friend. The brutal beating that hurled Danny Cade into eternity brought me immeasurable grief. Later when I had to serve as a prosecution witness in three successive murder trials, prayer saturated all my days, believe me—and I found that I did indeed forgive the three young criminals I faced. I grieved for them, wished good to them, and knew all the while that it was not *I* who was capable of forgiving but that Grace was coursing through its channels.

From that dire episode of my life I know firsthand that forgiveness can happen. I know further and intensely that "to forgive" is not at all the same as "to condone" or "to accept" or "to approve." Forgiven wrong is still a wrong and must be so regarded. Let me urge you to remember that principle always; we need to be very clear about it. That I felt warm, healing currents of forgiveness toward three young criminals did not take away the horror of their deed. Sometimes within family relationships, as in business or at school, we may too quickly say "Oh, that's okay" when a deed is not an "okay" but rather an egregious wrong. We must not condone what is wrong, must not call it a right.

Yet, hallelujah, the most egregious and bitter wrong can also become a *forgiven* wrong.

Specifically, whatever your father has done to damage you or disappoint you or deny you can through Grace become a forgiven wrong. Can you let retroactive love reach back through all your yesterdays?

Recently I found this small narrative in a little booklet called *Pathways to God*. (Small, but not small!) It is apropos on the nature of forgiveness. "Nearly a quarter of a century ago," wrote E. N. Barrows, "a young boy of six was sexually abused. The physical hurt of the experience was excruciating. The psychological hurt brought about by this offense was devastating. The emotional hurt caused by his parents' refusal to talk with him about the incident filled him with shame toward himself and hate for them.

"Twenty years of psychological and emotional hate filled the boy's life with darkness. Then one day a very wonderful, caring Christian man shared with him the love of Jesus Christ. As a young man he saw a flicker of light in his dark world. He accepted and experienced the light and forgiveness Jesus offered. Today, though he *remembers* the hurt and the hate of that childhood experience, he does not *feel* the hurt and hate. Today he is sharing the light of love and forgiveness in Jesus Christ with every person he can."

Is your commuter train slowing for a station? (Here, the fat yellow candle has guttered out and the telephone has been ringing; outside the blue jays are saluting morning with their blue-jay hallelujahs.)

Are you frowning and tapping fingers against your now-folded morning paper and muttering, "So I forgive. And tomorrow he'll make me angry again, or next week, or the next time I see him. . . . "

So?

So let's turn back to the red-printed columns and to the exuberant hyperbole of Matthew 18:22. "Shall I forgive this klutz of a brother of mine seven times?" asked grumbling Peter.

"Seven?" grinned Jesus. Surely he grinned a warm human grin as he said it. "Try seventy times seven, Pete!"

So.

Retroactive love for things past, anticipatory love for things future.

Anticipatory love, to be sure, may not be as neat and glib and easy as it might sound. Remember, it cost our Lord the cross. From that very cross, furthermore, he gave us the ultimate lesson in the nature of forgiveness when he cried out, "Father, forgive them, for they know not what they do."

Are you starting to pick up your brief case and topcoat? Your station is the next one?

Before your station comes, let's have another look back at the model prayer Jesus gave us in Matthew 6. Here, put your finger on his comments that immediately follow it. Have you noticed lately that "as we forgive" is the one phrase in the prayer for which he chose to add a comment? It's central, central to our own well-being. In a quick commuter-train paraphrase: "if you don't pour out retroactive love to other people, you will block up the love God is ready to give to you." Surely it is not so much a divine threat as a statement of impossibility; unforgiving, you simply cannot be a free, forgiven person.

You stand and step over toward the aisle, but reach back to grip my hand. Your face is alert, intense, expressive. "So," you murmur thoughtfully, "to forgive *anyone* is a prerequisite for the course, but to forgive a *father* is more like term papers and major exams, maybe? It's a crucial way to honor him. . . ."

The train sways into motion again. . . . Or you complete the forms in an Ohio employment office. . . . Or you resume your quiz-making in a California teachers' lounge. . . . May our Lord help you, as only he can, to forgive—

and to forgive—
and to forgive—
and to forgive.

11

TO HONOR *WHICH* FATHER?

Jeremy's face is like a jaunty mask whenever he passes a department store window featuring Father's Day gifts, whenever his high school announces a Father-Son event, whenever any speaker talks about acquiring wisdom from your father or about giving honor to a father. Sometimes Jeremy's quizzical-cynical eyebrows may quirk a little.

If you could talk with him long enough and quietly enough to hear the thoughts that are always jumping around behind Jeremy's quirky eyebrows, you might hear an agonized outcry. "My father? *Which* father? I've had three, and I don't have any, and whaddya expect me to do about it all? I'd like to know . . . I'd just like to know. . . ."

If your hand on Jeremy's tense shoulder were to encourage him to say a little more, he might stumble-mutter through a quick summary: his biological father was a casual boyfriend who dated a girl just long enough and ardently enough to make her Jeremy's mother. "I don't know one thing about him, and I don't wanta know. I suppose I get some of my looks from him and some of my aptitudes or lack of 'em, but there's no point in wondering, is there? Mom has never talked about him, and I'm not about to ask her any questions, that's for sure."

After the unknown Father #1, Jeremy's mother was married for a while to a Father #2, whom he remembers with tentative uncertainties. Then a divorce happened. He remembers tears and angry voices and the move to an apartment. Later on, Father #3. A wedding with lots of happy excitement and gruff-kind promises made to him and having a father with him at the P.T.A. events for a while. Then new kinds of anger, new tears, new quarrels, another new apartment. Three fathers, and no father.

* * *

Instead of someone talking with a Jeremy, maybe you are a Jeremy. There are Jeremys all across America: two fathers, three fathers, four fathers, three and yet none.

Just a few weeks ago a Jeremy's mother's voice telephoned me from a distant state. After reading something I had written, she called to pour out some queries about the plight of her soul. I had written about being single, and she is now single for a fourth time: three marriages, three divorces. We talked and talked; we voiced prayer words across the long distance wires, and a yearning prayer for her sons twinges again inside me now. Three fathers, and no father.

To her sons, to any Jeremy, what can one say while Jeremy faces his *now*?

* * *

Well, first, Jeremy, remember that it's *your* life. Other people can give you ideas and suggestions, but you are the one who grabs for handholds and pushes through thorns on your own climbing trails. We want to help you, but nobody else can ever know exactly what the ledges are like where you are right now. Collect climbing tools and counsel from anyone and everyone, and then use your own best judgment. Will you?

If you are still seeing sometimes a former stepfather or a former-former stepfather, can you pick up some cues from him and from Mom and from the social situations about how dignity and courage and courtesy will instruct you to act? They're good instructors: dignity and courage and courtesy. Listen well where they speak!

When you think back to other times, Jeremy, and remember Father #2 or Father #3, can you collect some negative counsel from them? Did their lives show traits that you never, never, never want to emulate? (Ed's anger? Ken's inability to hear anyone else in a discussion? Joe's selfishness? Tom's shiftless ways?) One year I signed up with great excitement and anticipation for a summer course offered in a pleasant town near splendid mountain scenery. Well, I enjoyed the mountains, but the course itself proved to be woefully disappointing. I came home able to tell my friends, however, that I had learned a good deal—I had learned some things about how *not* to teach. In a similar way, as you look back, can you learn *not* and *not* and *not* about living from those temporary transient fathers?

Another thought, if you are a Jeremy.

Can you be adroit and energetic in borrowing fathers? It's a useful maneuver for many, many sorts and types of people, but especially for you Jeremy-people.

Your history teacher may never know that you are borrowing him to admire during your third-hour class and sixth-hour study hall every day. No matter! Your coach. Your preacher. Two or three neighbors with whom you trade jobs. Sometimes you'll borrow them only inside your own imaginative head. Sometimes you'll borrow them for "how to" sessions with tools or for an evening at a ball game.

Are you lucky enough to have an uncle or older cousin or grandfather you can talk with and "borrow" sometimes? Maybe one of them can help you sort out whether you should now be giving some continuing attention to your Father #2 and your Father #3. Whether, and how, and what kind of attention. And good strands of fatherness, if we can call it that, may often be happily woven into your life, Jeremy, through even brief bits of time with Uncle Pete or Grandpa George.

I just spoke of "Fatherness." It reminds me of some philosophical speculations from one of the most brilliant mortals who ever thought and talked and wrote upon this earth. Old Plato the philosopher, who lived in Greece from about 427 to 347 B.C. He pondered about one concept I think has some mileage in it for all the Jeremys around us—and indeed for many another person who finds a father somehow hard to honor.

Without going into a full lecture from Philosophy 101A, let me just mention that Plato pondered about all that we see around us in the physical world. He saw earthly things as imperfect and changing copies of "Ideas" or "Forms" that exist beyond our temporal now. The Idea "beauty" is; we see copies and fragments of it. The Idea "good" is; we see changing, imperfect representations of it.

Now—still pausing far short of Philosophy 101A—I think we could suggest that fatherness *is*. Some young people see a great deal of "fatherness" (kindness, integrity, firmness, honesty, willingness to instruct, fidelity, affection) in their own human fathers. Some see very little.

If, like Jeremy, one has had a procession of father figures who truly did not manifest much "fatherness," Jeremy can still keep watching for examples of it all around him and choosing the ideals he himself will affirm, live by, incorporate into his own inmost being.

Imagine parts of a day in Jeremy's life.

Alarm clock. Sounds of angry yelling in the apartment upstairs. Not fatherness, that!

He walks through the living room, notices a photo of Father #3 still on the mantel. Nice eyebrows, virile beard, pleasant smile. Yes, visually, fatherness.

Breakfast. Mom talks about materials Pastor Jones sent home for the youth conference next week; Jeremy is to ride with him. (Oh, good. He remembered about me. He cares. Fatherness.)

School bus. Driver is brusque, kind, raucous, rough of speech. Plus and minus. Some fatherness.

Classes. Dr. Schmid is unreasonable, temper-tense. (A very imperfect copy of the fatherness idea!) Dr. Wilson is brawny-muscular in stature, firm and demanding in assignments; tough love encased in tweeds. Now there is fatherness!

Evening. Jeremy relaxes for a while and watches "Little House on the Prairie" or "The Waltons" or "Different Strokes" or some other popular program; he evaluates, evaluates, evaluates. There's fatherness! Yes, there. No, oh no. That one is fatherness betrayed and besmeared. But there. And there. And there.

Courage is fatherness. Trusting one's children is fatherness. . . . ideals in action. . . faith. . . gentleness in boots and flannels. . . integrity, no matter what. . . solicitude for women. . . moral rectitude. . . .

Handsome hair and handsome chin line? Well, maybe. Nice optional fixtures, actually. Fatherness is much deeper than hair, deeper than bone structure.

Will this be a guideline for you, Jeremy?

Whenever a man shows you "fatherness"—whether he's known to your associates as your ex-stepfather or your ex-ex-stepfather, your great-uncle or a janitor, your boss or a shoe salesman—you can joyfully salute the fatherness in him. So to salute, however you perform it, will strengthen you and be a wholesome honor to him.

12

A CUP OF SUBTLE POISON

Stop. Put it down!

It looks like an ordinary cup of breakfast coffee you are drinking, but it is a cup of subtle poison: coffee mixed full to the brim with self-pity.

Justifiable, yes.

(You aren't welcome at his apartment . . . . He deserted Mom and you . . . . He is a dictator toward you . . . . He never did want you . . . . He plays favorites, and you're not a favorite . . . . He doesn't come to see you . . . . He could help you with college expenses, but he won't think of it . . . . All of the above, and bitter others beyond them. . . .)

Justifiable, yes.

But self-pity becomes poison to the lips that sip it.

"Poor me" is a natural outcry. You have been wounded. Painful, vile, and dismal events have happened, and they do not go away. Yet the cry of "poor me" indulged in and lived with will constantly send new devastation out into your present and your future.

Have you watched physically handicapped persons enough to know that it is a principle of our human situation? Or elderly persons, now limited by life? Or divorced persons? "Poor me" tends to block all the flow of love both from the whimperer and toward him. No matter how justifiable, "poor me" tends to repulse one's associates like a foul and fetid B. O. of the personality, or like the halitosis all the mouthwash commercials warn us against. All we see of human experience convinces us: pain may stretch the heart toward new and nobler dimensions, but fondled pain, self-pitying pain, inevitably shrivels and diminishes and weakens it.

When one has known and is knowing an agony, life becomes an immensely consequential multiple-choice test. Have you chanced yet to read Viktor Frankl's book, *Man's Search for Meaning*? From the horrors of the Nazi death camps he came to the conviction that the ultimate human value was the chance to choose one's responses. In your present circumstance you can choose. You are choosing. You may complain loudly and audibly, trying to find some worth among your associates by your "poor me" recitals. You may be more silent about it but whimper inwardly all the while. Or you may accept and bear and grow.

That last choice may sound glib, but it is never glibly lived nor glibly experienced when courage grapples with pain. (Not even when the pain is far less pervasive, less devastating than yours.) And self-pity must be faced; it simply must.

How?

What are the alternatives?

Well, in any life they will intertwine and overlap, but let's consider some principles that would seem to be at work.

It is good to recognize the reality of a situation, to face it, to accept it. Emotions and circumstances must be called by right names before one can stiffen the shoulders to bear them, but then the accepting, the bearing can begin. In the phrasing of an ancient writer, the sufferer comes to assert, "Woe is me for my hurt! my wound is grievous: but I said, Truly this is a grief, and I must bear it."

As time goes on, as you set new goals and meet new endeavors, the accepting and the bearing can happen more and more fully as you refuse to give way to self-pity.

Sometimes it may be heartening to remind yourself of others who have met a great grief (maybe your very kind of grief) and have nevertheless moved forward with life rather than continually giving in to those draining, weakening poisons of self-pity. Michelangelo, for instance. Recently when I was reading a book on that great genius in the Time-Life series on artists, I was startled to learn that his father was characterized as being "filled with vanity," a person of "mean-mindedness," and of "complete indifference to the needs and dreams of others." Michelangelo Buonorotti, one imagines, could have wasted his creative years in a "poor me, my wretched father!" kind of lamentation, but he had other things to do.

Rather a different individual, but also one worth thinking about. When Dick Cavett interviewed animal trainer Gunther Gebel-Williams, very eminent in his field today, the audience learned that Gebel-Williams had been separated from his father as a child in Europe during World War II and then abandoned by his mother when he was twelve. When Cavett offered a sensitive word of commiseration, Gebel-Williams quickly shrugged it away. No, he said, his circumstances had made him "tough enough to face life."

So the griefs had happened. The important thing, he implied, was to pick up and go on from there.

And I have to think, on an infinitely smaller scale, of a motto we developed once when I spent a summer traveling with a college musical group (as their speaker, chaperon, and general assistant) and small frictional episodes would happen in our schedule or with our weary old station wagon: "Well, it has happened. How can we make the best of it?" People who outgrow self-pity are always asking: How can we make the best of it?

Along with a Michelangelo and Gebel-Williams, might you find some chuckles and pluck in one of the old Horatio Alger stories? His fiction may have been trite and romanticized, but he certainly nudged his readers toward elbowing away this cup of subtle poison we're talking about.

Having set some goals and squared your shoulders toward them (in a daily exercise that will also be lifelong; I don't want to make it sound like a sentimental hocus-pocus), probably it will help if you will resolutely affirm the good things that come to you. Sometimes they will be trivial little blessings. Sometimes they will be momentous ones that can be ignored unless you push yourself to notice and to affirm them. The old Sunday school song urging us to count our many blessings, "name them one by one," is validity and therapy and valuable realism.

Perhaps you have heard a thousand times the often-quoted motto, " I complained about my shoes until I met the man who had no feet." But it deserves yet more quoting. Do you have feet? Do you have ears and eyes? Do you have a friend? A job? An education, or part of one, already? What do you have? You must have sensitivity enough that you can hurt. How can you make that sensitivity into yet more of a blessing?

That last query leads, inevitably, to a next principle. An antidote for self-pity, often and often, is to reach out to someone who has different woes from your own. They may be proportionately tiny woes, but in swabbing iodine on scratches you can help the hurt of your amputation. The practical daily deeds can be very therapeutic. To visit a friend who is down with pneumonia. To help with a recreation project in a prison. To take a senior citizen with rheumatism out for a drive. To write a letter to a cousin or an uncle.

I pause to think about Dick for a moment. If I read the weather signs in his life accurately, Dick lives under deep and constant clouds of self-pity. Thunderclouds. With lightning often present. He has seemed truly to hate and resent and despise his father ever since the latter's divorce, and now all those emotions and the newer events of his life have Dick pretty constantly sighing "poor me." Friends and his other relatives wonder how he could he helped. At the risk of oversimplifying everything in Dick's life, I'd venture an opinion: that if he would pour himself into avid and deliberately cheerful correspondence with those other relatives, trying to make *their* woes fewer, he could gradually (but briskly) become a very different and much happier person.

The impulse to help someone else may continue therapeutically right on through life. Did you chance to read an article about Senator Denton of Alabama in *Time* magazine for June 8, 1981? Denton, we learn, is a crusader on behalf of family life in his political involvements and commitments, and the stated reason for his crusading is that he is "still preoccupied" with his father, who caused him to have a "rootless" childhood. The article identifies his father as "a womanizer, a real estate speculator, a onetime bookie." Scars. Anguish. Old pain. But in the senator's life it has all undergone a chemical change and produced continuing service to society. From pain to action rather than to brooding has evidently been his pattern.

The *Time* article implies further that Senator Denton has come to his present roles through his affection for his wife and children. In reading about him I think of a widely-known poet I heard read a powerful poem about his boyish hatred for his neglectful father. Later I asked him if he could make any comments on how he had worked through the bitter emotions, and he replied that the healings for him had come in large measure from the new affections that came with the years: his lovely wife, his daughters.

For you who are tilting the cups of poison across the breakfast tables, there is not now a therapy just like Denton's or just like the poet's. No wife, no children. Not now.

But the principle is larger. Giving new affection can always help to work healings when old affections have been crushed or amputated or stolen. Always. And there are people around you who need your affection now. Maybe the relationships are of sorts that will make affection seem very trickle-small in comparison with the great rivers of filial affection that you would like to be giving and receiving, but trickles and creeklets can be very, very important.

Your brother. Your sister. (Are they as devastated as you and needing rivers also?) Cousins. Uncles. The kids in a Boy Scout troop to whom you are a Mr. Wonderful. Lonesome neighbors you could have in for a chili supper. Someone at the office who is a hurting parent as well as a computer programmer.

In continual and creative ways can you give love and give love and give love? Unstintingly. Undemandingly. Experimentally. Creatively. It's the antidote for poisons, armor against demons.

Since that word "love" has been so twisted and mangled by Hollywood and sordid fiction and TV, should we add a modifier and urge you toward wholesome love?

No one could make any wild guess as to how many young people have accepted illicit sex as a flawed substitute for parental affection within the past decade or so. However many, it is tragedy indeed for each and each. Self-pity that pulls you toward a welcoming but unblessed bed is a particularly vicious form of that emotion.

In utter contrast, a permanent refuge from every "poor me" impulse that can ever happen is available, always, in the love of Christ Jesus himself. It is always utterly safe to tell him about the bitter stresses. In any circumstance you could not find courage to tell to any friend or counselor, he is refuge and he is strength. He was on earth as "a man of sorrows and acquainted with grief," and he is acquainted with the utmost depths and crevices of your present grief. In the paradox of Christian experience he knows already about you and yet he welcomes you to tell him about yourself. Tell him! Daily. Sometimes hourly. Sometimes moment after moment, while you are in the midst of desk work and jangling telephones. Tell him!

Sometimes, too, you will want to ask him specifically for diagnosis. It's a clear fact of human experience that most of us do not easily admit to self-pity. Does anyone ever leave school or office or social event announcing that he is going home for a good ol' binge of self-pity? But it catches us, invades us, attacks us. We would say we are just "facing the facts," perhaps, or just "thinking things over," but we're actually giving in to this virulent emotion. We need the one who knows us utterly to help us know ourselves.

Have you turned back recently to Isaiah 53, from which I was quoting a couple of paragraphs ago? When your anger and dismay and sense of loss become most anguished, it's a good passage to read again, again, and yet again. "Surely he hath borne our griefs." Ours. Yours. The present ones. He has borne them. "And carried our sorrows." Yours. Whatever their dimensions! "And with his stripes we are healed." Another translation says "his bruises." When your spirit is bruised black and purple, can you remember it? His bruises make it possible for our bruisings to be healed.

Minutes ago I reread an aching, angry, tense letter from Joe. I was glad to get it when it came, and yet not glad. His dad's new marriage still rankles terribly, and Joe's comments are virulent. He has been sipping (or gulping) from this subtle poison, and he doesn't seem to know that he has. I wonder if Joe has a faithful friend who could say to him all we have just been talking about, whom Joe could then trust to cry "Hey, watch it" when he starts reaching again for the cup.

In any circumstance of life it is a poison. For all the Joes of America it is a poison with devastating aftereffects. Put it down!

13

A WORD FROM THE NIGHT

Last night my mind climbed up from the deep depths for a moment, a very memorable moment. It was at 2:00 A.M., perhaps, or 3:00. I didn't flick on a light nor even stir enough to notice what the classical music station I had left on was sending softly from my radio. In the one-tenth-awake moment Mind prayed a silent prayer: "Lord Jesus, what do you want me to tell them?" In the next seconds, even as Mind was sliding back toward deep slumber, an answer was welling up as a long-ago memorized verse spoke in firm cadences: "When my father and my mother forsake me, then the Lord will take me up."

At 5:30 or so when I heard a Bruckner symphony playing and caught shimmering silver trumpet tones, I thought about it: "The Lord will take me up." Later as suavely modulated and remote voices of announcers talked about diplomats, the president's advisers, the wind chill factor's being up to minus eight, I again thought about it: "The Lord will take me up."

Minutes ago I read from the resonant poetry of old Isaiah: "How beautiful upon the mountains are the feet of him that bringeth good tidings, that publisheth peace; that bringest good tidings of good, that publisheth salvation. . . . " I smiled. Today for once in my life my feet are going to be beautiful! Today this weary old Olympia portable might be wearing a halo like the ones medieval painters imagined for their portraits; it has "tidings of good" to announce.

I'd like to shout it to about a million people all across America: Yes, you are forsaken, but look! You are being sought out!

More than any census could possibly record, America is a nation filled with father-seekers. That I believe.

Sometimes when a soldier picks up another beer and another and another, he is trying to stifle the father-yearning that will not go away. Sometimes when a high school boy accepts marijuana for the first time, or the hundredth time, it isn't marijuana that he really craves but the security of Dad-and-me, the renewal of a splintered identity. Sometimes when businessmen quarrel with their wives or say rude words to their bosses or kick the dog or curse the moon, they are really whimpering, "Father! My father. . . . I didn't mean it, Dad. Come

home, come home, come home. . . . Father, I need you. . . . I'm lost
and broken without you, Dad. . . . Oh, father. My father, my father,
my father."

Probably the seeking is often at such deep and obscurely hidden
levels that even a psychiatrist could hardly find it, but it is there.
Along with all the racial memories of sons striding beside fathers to
hunt bison or trap tigers, it is there. Misted in the legends of campfires
and oxcarts, of Trojan wars and the Crusades, it is there. The echo of
"Help me here, my father"—as spoken at the building of the Great
Wall of China, in launching Viking prows, dipping first primitive nets
through blue Mediterranean waters, hewing tough Anglo-Saxon
oak—sounds through every regional dialect in modern America.

Often it happens among us, to be sure, that a son is the forsaker.
Many a modern man, like an ancient King David, sometimes must
mourn for the Absalom whose life he would gladly have bought with
his own. But my "good tidings" for this day are to the myriad sons
who are forsaken ones.

Forsaken.

Maybe you have always been forsaken—God pity you!—because
your father didn't want children at all and counted you a hindrance to
his pursuit of happiness. He wanted your mother to be his continual
playmate, and you were a resented intrusion. He lived with you while
you were small, and yet emotionally he did not live with you. You
were forsaken. (Remembering. I think of a wretched young woman I
once saw at a church camp and of her husband's furious jealousy
against their sons. He sat with them, bought meals for them, chauf-
feured them around in his car, but oh, they were forsaken, forsaken,
forsaken.)

Maybe you were the emotional outcast because his favoritisms
preferred the others. He adored your sisters' blonde ringlets and ignored your darker stubble? He praised your brother's skill with tools
and derided your efforts?

Again, remembering. I was guiding a room full of sophomores in
discussions of *Adam Bede*, and we were talking about how Lisbeth
Bede continually demanded the attention of her favorite, Adam, how
she continually disdained the affection of her younger son, Seth. "It
really does happen in families sometimes, doesn't it?" I asked. "Have
you ever known a family where the situation was something like
this?" And toward the back of the room a spasm of horrible pain flicked
across one handsome face. Ben nodded in response, said something
from the edge of his mouth to the student beside him. And I knew he
was seeing his brother Bobby in George Eliot's character Adam. I
would have called Ben more winsome than his older brother, but ap-

parently the family had lauded and exalted taller Bobby for their twenty years together, and Ben felt himself deeply forsaken.

Or perhaps you were forsaken and are forsaken over and over and over by the way your father puts the demands of his work ahead of you?

You know the shape of his suitcases, but you don't know the shape of his affection. He goes back to the office night after night, or he goes out with clients. "Sh-h-h. Daddy's in his study and we mustn't bother him." Telephone, telephone, telephone. School programs, and Daddy is out of town. "Next week, Joe; we'll fish next week, for sure." "Some day next summer I'll take you to the zoo; that's a promise, Joe." But you didn't, and he didn't. Your recital? Nope, it can't be done. Your grad school admission. "Dad would write, Joe, but he's awfully busy right now; you know how it is with his job. . . . "

Yes. You know how it is. He keeps his job and earns promotions, but you are one of the forsaken ones.

Or maybe you gulp a different flavor of the bitter beverage. Maybe, in fact, you have been forsaken through his unremitting disapproval of you. Through long long chapters of his commands and demands and rebukes, through shoutings that alternated with icy anger (splinters of ice moving up your vertebrae; frost patterns on the inside of your skull), you have not been able to please him. Sometimes, in truth, you tried to please him and sometimes you did not. Looking back, he always seemed insatiable in what he wanted from you, but you realize now that he was probably more reasonable than he seemed. But his disapproval led to more disapproval and to your violent rebellions. ("Okay, I'll give him something to be mad about this time!") And finally a last anger came. When you were arrested for drunken driving? When you told him that you and Suzie were getting married anyway, even though he raged at you and forbade you to think of it? He couldn't approve of a Suzie in *his* family, he said, so you quietly walked out of his family for good. Was that it? Or was his ultimate disapproval when you took the job in Chicago after he had insisted you should stay near him and Mom in upstate New York?

He disapproved, and you are forsaken.

Or yours is the other searing pain, the day-long and night-long pain, the pain that stains all skies and smogs over all landscapes: divorce. He got a divorce from Mom. He left you.

It still stuns. It's like burning ten thousand fingers at once on ten thousand different matches. It's like sewer stench. It's like breaking teeth on nutshells, breaking about a million teeth. It's like the sensation of drowning, that time when you were seven, but this goes on

and goes on and goes on; your head never comes out of the water.
    Divorce.
    You visit him sometimes and try to be nice to his new wife, but you are forsaken. You are forsaken.
    I pick up my oldest Bible, once rebound and falling apart again. Yellowy pages, much underlined. I thumb to Psalm 27:10. There it is: the verse Mind heard at 2:00 or 3:00 A.M.: "When my father and my mother forsake me, then the Lord will take me up." The Hebrew wording, says the margin, would be more nearly "the Lord will gather me." I like that. I visualize great comforting arms reaching out to gather us toward himself. Ultimate Care takes us into his care when the other caring has dissolved—for whatever reason it has dissolved. Whatever and whatever and whatever.
    All the father-seekers in America, then, are not ultimately lonely, nor all the father-seekers on our round earth.
    Or, more precisely, we do not need to be lonely. We would understand, I think, from the whole texture of all the biblical prom- ises, that God will "take up" the one who allows himself to be taken. Years ago I heard a small sentence spoken by a voice I respected. It may have been Dr. B. H. Pearson speaking to our youth camp group at Cawker City, Kansas, when I was a teen-ager there. "God is a gentleman," said the thoughtful voice. "He does not come in where he is not invited." That dictum leads us straight over to the resonant voice of Christ himself as recorded in Revelation 3:20: "Behold, I stand at the door, and knock; if any man hear my voice, and open the door, I will come in to him, and will sup with him, and he with me."
    Can you grip the Revelation verse and the Psalm verse firmly in your two hands? Can you start exploring what it will mean in the course of your life to be one God Almighty has "taken up"? Yesterday you were a forsaken one; today you are a chosen one, taken into his particular care!
    Can you think of it often while you shave or jog or drive to work, while you wait for an elevator or jostle your way into a subway train? The Lord will take you up. It would be entirely appropriate, I think, to hear the future tense verb as having all the tenses implicit within it: He will take, he is taking, he has taken, he will have taken, he will be taking, he will have been taking. It's a spacious verb; you can't possibly jostle your elbows against the edges of it, nor touch the height of it from any ladder!
    So what does that mean, in the daily practicalities we live among?
    Ask him!
    Guidance.
    The sure knowledge of his immense love.

A recognition of your especial worth, to him. He values you, as you, because you are you.

"*When my father and my mother forsake me, then the Lord* will *take me up.*"

14

TO CHANGE THE FILTERS?

For the past half hour I have been leafing through a book on photography. One two-page spread is so dramatic that I wish you could look over my shoulder and exclaim with me. On the left a handsome full-page photo in carefully modulated authentic color of Michelangelo's great marble statue of Moses; on the right six small prints of the same photo, each in badly distorted color. "Too much cyan. Too much magenta. Too much yellow," say the successive captions. "Too much red. Too much green. Too much blue." Each print carries its own repulsive dismay to observing eyes—especially when the eyes, like mine, have looked at Michelangelo's famous statue from almost elbow-near observing angles and appreciate fully the authentic color here on the left.

The photography book is talking about color filters that can be used to correct imbalances in lighting from fluorescent light or "manufacturing variations" in film or other circumstances. A camera records what is in front of it—but it cannot always see accurately; in this "too much red" print, for example, one would think a big fire was blazing in the church and casting a ruddy glow over the hair and beard and chin and shoulders of the statue.

While I look at these six faulty pictures of the Moses, I have to ponder about the faulty photographs our human eyes sometimes keep on taking. How often should "He is . . ." be more accurately phrased, "As I perceive him to be, he is . . . "?

Sometimes when we see a grade school teacher, a junior high friend, a neighbor across the alley, an employer, a cousin, are we seeing through light that needs corrective cyan or magenta filters? Maybe, for example, you think your new roommate is haughty and discover gradually that instead he is painfully shy. Maybe you think a teacher dislikes you—and find out, to your surprise, that he is being very careful not to create any petty jealousies among your classmates by showing how very much he values you. And so on.

Inaccurate information or past experiences can often fit wrong circlets of color over the lenses of the mind. Have you watched it happen?

An episode from several years ago still chides me sharply as I remember how it did happen, once. While I waited in a line at the college cafeteria one day, I noticed a student who had not removed his very visible cap; I was surprised at his lack of courtesy, according to that year's definite courtesy codes. "Well," I thought, "we're still in the entry lounge. He'll take it off when he comes to the serving area." But he didn't. "He'll take it off when he is seated," I thought. "He won't be so rude as to wear it at the table." But he left it on and added to his flaunting of the codes by wearing it right over to the table where a professor was being seated. And then within a few minutes of conversation I found the lens filters to be flipping very rapidly. Bill has sustained an ugly scalp wound, and his doctor wanted it to have contact for a while with air rather than with bandages. Bill was wearing a porous cap in order to keep the rest of us from being nauseated by looking at his raw flesh, not to insult us.

The filters. The faulty perceptions.

How often are tensions with fathers aggravated grievously because of the not always-accurate ways we perceive our fathers? Can it happen?

I'm thinking about a family situation that a friend described to me with some intensity just recently. It's a family he knows well. (Call them the Jamiesons.) They have two daughters. When the girls were in their teens, Janice—says my friend—perceived her father as very solicitous. She appreciated his concern, accepted it, and maintained a warmly loving relationship. Now married, Janice is more than happy to have Dad visit her home, and his affection still brightens her life.

Her sister Marilyn saw through very different filters. (Blue? Magenta? Cyan?) What Janice saw as *solicitude* in Mr. Jamieson, Marilyn resented as *domination*. Fierce dramas followed, as Marilyn rebelled against "domination" and Mr. Jamieson became more and more concerned about her. More of solicitude, which Marilyn saw in yet deeper magenta tones of "domination." She felt it, says my friend, as a crushing weight that threatened to suffocate her, and she rebelled even more violently both against him and against the God whom she resented as a cosmic projection of Mr. Jamieson. Now in her thirties, Marilyn is struggling to be right with God—and apparently, from my friend's account, she is making valiant efforts at last to twist those old filter clasps.

Can you take a deep breath—maybe shudder-deep—and think hard? Can you ponder it day and night and between times for a while? Have your perceptions of your father sometimes been inaccurate? Have you looked through dark blue filtering gelatin at his moods, his commands, his personal traits, his ways of discipline?

You can't become omniscient by trying for new vantage points; you may not even become mini-iscient! But the effort is worth making.

Might it be useful if you would ask a few people whom you trust to check you out? If you could slowly, quietly, thoughtfully, ask a pastor, an uncle, a neighbor, a classmate about how other eyes perceive Dad, might their observations clarify and help to adjust your own perceptions?

If you spend enough time in the photographic darkrooms, you may come to an uneasy certainty that you have not been seeing your father as accurately, as fairly, as truly as you might. Then, how to change the reflexes of twenty years? (How to release the filter clasps? What adjusting filter rightly to insert?)

Well, to start with, how about considering some of "the power of positive thinking"? Whatever your total evaluations of a Norman Vincent Peale, there can be great and wholesome usefulness in the process when you "accentuate the positive."

Reach for some paper.

Almost anything on earth can be described by neutral adjectives, or by commendatory adjectives, or by pejorative adjectives, depending upon the observer. To John's friends he is *thrifty*; to less appreciative eyes he is *stingy*. The same person may be *"hot-headed"* or *"so warmly impulsive,"* depending upon who labels him. And so on. How about jotting down some phrases you often tend to apply (either aloud or very silently) to your father. Then put beside them the terms a different filter could honestly record?

Now, keep going.

In anger and in the habits built by anger we always tend to focus on what frustrates, annoys, or repels us. What are his winsome traits that you tend to forget and ignore? Can you widen and clarify your perception of reality—of good reality? Keep the paper in front of you, and keep jotting. What in him do you appreciate, does anyone appreciate? What are his strengths? Has your perception sometimes been like a line drawing rather than a photograph? Has it left out some beauty and depth and dimension that are actually there, although pretty habitually ignored?

After having thought, can you make some creative efforts to become verbal, to express your appreciation for what you now see to be visibly present? A small "fan mail" note saluting Dad's perseverance in killing dandelions last Saturday, or his enthusiasm at tennis yesterday, or his chivalry in greeting your latest date—or any one of a thousand other affirmations—might be a wonderfully deft filter adjustment.

And from appreciation on to outright gratitude made explicitly known?

Human error abounds, and it abounds among fathers. I know that, you know it, we all know it. Yet many good traits, many solicitudes, many generosities also abound. To say the frequent and specific "thank you" can help to change the bitter toward the better. When did you last thank Dad warmly for groceries that his paycheck purchased? For his counsel about colleges? For use of the family TV set? For teaching you how to fling a football? For your bedroom—if you have one; for a shower stall, a guitar, a bicycle, an auto, a baseball—if you have one. And so on.

I finger the photography book again, glance at an "Exposure and Filter Compensation" chart, and wonder about some rather different camera effects of inaccurate perceptions that we sometimes perpetrate. Unlike teen-ager Marilyn Jamieson, who saw her father as grimmer than he was, do some of our filters or our retouching devices try to see a father as impossibly heroic, impossibly noble? If a home has operated too firmly on principles of "Father knows best" and "Don't argue with your father!" and of hero-worship, disillusionments will eventually come. And they may be jarringly painful when they come. Yet accurate vision needs to be achieved, even if it comes about through painful processes. (The Moses statue really looks much better in its natural color tones than in any of the exaggerated tints.) To perceive clearly, honestly, accurately is surely a worthy goal; to adjust the filters for correct photos, whatever that may mean. And then, on from there!

For filial relationships as well as for more general topics he was discussing, Matthew Arnold expressed a high ideal when he urged his nineteenth century readers to "see life steadily and see it whole." Can you obey him in challenging new ways?

15

WHEN YOUR MOTHER MAKES IT HARDER . . .

For five centuries or so British and American people have been reading or singing or quoting with deep tremors of emotion an old Scottish ballad, "Edward, Edward." In its terse dialogue a mother asks her son, Edward, about the blood dripping from his sword and about his dire sadness. "I've killed my hawk," he tells her, but she pushes the inquiry. "I've killed my red-roan steed," he evades next, but she still questions, and he confesses:

> "O I have killed my father dear,
> Alas, and woe is me O!"

The mother continues her questioning. "What, then, will happen to his manor buildings?" "Let them stand until they fall down," cries Edward. "Your bairns and your wife?" "Let them beg, as they can."

Then in the chilling final stanza the mother puts one more in-quiry: "What will you leave to your own dear mother?" And the young man cries out in a voice that has chilled our ancestral marrow down through the centuries,

> "The curse of hell from me shall ye bear, Mother, Mother,
> The curse of hell from me shall ye bear,
> Such counsels you gave to one O."

One woman in medieval Scotland set her son against his father, and we still hear the echo of her crime, of his horror. But her guilt was not totally different, actually, from what is happening daily in a million homes across America as fathers are being stabbed and slashed in other ways than with a medieval sword. Too many a modern Ed-ward is receiving "such counsels" against a father.

Sometimes it happens without any plan or intention; it just hap-pens, as a mother's pain or desperation of turmoil spills over onto her children.

A widely-known American writer told me, for example, about the bitter episodes of his boyhood. When his father, a traveling salesman, would come home at infrequent intervals, there would be harsh parental quarrels, mostly about always-sparse money, and Bill tended to side with his mother. More quarrels, more siding with his mother. More quarrels. More siding with his mother. And increasing, durable hate against his father, with scars that many intervening years since his father's death have not totally healed.

More than she knew, Bill's mother made it hard and harder for Bill ever to honor a father.

Rob's mother put dirks and swordlets into Rob's hands, too, though in very different ways. Rob's mother was a brilliantly successful professional woman. Extroverted, ambitious, energetic, she always tended to swirl other people into her wake in any community. She was genuinely fond of Rob's father, but Mr. J's gentle dreaminess vexed her and his occasional impracticalities angered her. So Rob grew up hearing barbed humor and household tirades and impatient scorn. To jibe at Dad, not honor him, was a way of life his boyhood often knew.

Max's mother. While she was falling out of love and dating other men and planning toward the divorce, she often yelled at her husband in the hearing of her children, often derided him, often reviewed his various faults. As the divorce came nearer, she tried to justify her own actions by "talking things over" with the children. Since the divorce she has continued to "talk things over." And Max now defies his father and quarrels with him and repudiates him until his friends wonder how things will ever end.

* * *

Whether you are closely like a Bill or a Rob or a Max, does having a *mother* sometime in some ways make it harder for you to honor a *father*?

In St. Paul's phrase, such things ought not so to be.

We realize that honor to father and to mother *should* be beautifully inseparable and utterly intertwined. We affirm that every wife *should* cherish her husband beyond all other men, in every moment, every episode, every situation of her married life. You feel with deep, yearning certainties that your father *should* be your tutor in all chivalry toward your mother, not her adversary nor her victim. But we live in a fallen world, and the bitter taste of Eden's fruit is upon all our tongues—except as God's grace intervenes and keeps on intervening.

How are you to react, how are you to cope, when Mom makes it hard for you to honor Dad?

Some thoughts, some observations, some comments, some suggestions. Some principles, first.

. . . Can you realize and remember that any marriage is in some measure an utter mystery to all outsiders? A marriage is complex, contradictory, an intricate blending of ecstasies and despairs, needs and fulfillments. Your parents are "one flesh," and each *is* the other, veritably.

So, can you stand back from the mystery and let it happen? Can you trust the mystery and refrain from taking sides within it? Recently I heard a genial bishop declare that he probably understands his lovely wife less now, after forty good years of matrimony, than he did when he was dating her. Mystery. Like an electric power plant any marriage carries its signboards: "High voltage. No admission. Keep out." That's only one part of the truth, of course, but don't ever forget that it's a part.

. . . A corollary, then. Don't be too sure, ever, that you understand your mother's emotions about your father. What sounds to you like flippant scorn she's tossing at him may be about three-fourths adoration, and about two-thirds nostalgic private language between them.

. . . And yet, dishonesty is not demanded of you, or of anyone else, in facing a situation. You may need to speak some unpleasant truths before progress can happen: to yourself, to Mom, to siblings, to a counselor. Truth, honesty, candor within a family are often like iodine or Lysol or Merthiolate within a clinic. If Mom is a female Archie Bunker and treats Dad like a "Dingbat," well—that's what she is. If she says grace at the table and then talks in the tones of shrill profanity for all the rest of the meal—well, that's what she has done. "Let's face it" may be a beginning point for new clarity and new therapy.

. . . Within the stresses and decidings of family life do you sometimes feel pulled apart by the contradictions of "Honor your father" and "Honor your mother"? Are there times when you cannot honor both at once?

Maybe on any given occasion your responsibility will become crystal-clear as you discern that one seems to be on the side of the angels in this episode and one definitely is not. (Reaching that discernment won't happen in the blinking of an eyelash; don't expect that!)

If there aren't ethical issues to clarify things, if it's an absolute tossup, I wouldn't hesitate to say that you'd do well to follow the priority in the Sinai order. It was no accident or casual circumstance, I think, which put "Honor your father" at the beginning of the sentence. Ideally it's always in a hyphenated sense: "Honor-your-father-and-your-mother." If the hyphens have irreparably fallen away, why not take the command as it stands? Honor him. With everyone you can get to help you—especially with Mom, whenever it can happen—honor him.

. . . Fairness is important. Playing by the rules. The "Yes, but . . . " in a discussion. Fair to him, fair to her.

Do most boys, like Bill, tend sometimes to side with Mom when quarrels resound? Too much, too often, too unreasoningly, do they side with Mom, even in small episodes? Do others, junior-sized male chauvinists, unthinkingly side with Dad in any disagreement?

Whatever the initial tendency, to be fair is a worthy goal; it deserves your continual effort.

* * *

With those principles before us, let's think about some kinds of action you might initiate if yours is one of those homes where Mom makes it harder to honor Dad. (And, realistically, is there any unit of three persons in which a *two* do not sometimes join together against a *one*?)

Some suggestions may be more useful if you are now fourteen than if you are twenty-four or thirty-four or forty-four—but at any age at all, perhaps there will be ideas here to try on and work from and adapt. I hope so!

Idea #1. If Mom has acquired habits of derogation, can you make a real effort to develop habits of *praise*? If she's a little like Rob's mother—if she laughs with sharp-edged scorn over Dad's ineptitudes at golf or carpentry or the barbecue grill can you make a happy game with yourself of supplying specific little household accolades?

"Hey, Dad, Uncle George really enjoyed your stories at dinner last night. . . ."

"Your necktie is just the right color to make your eyes twinkle. . . ."

"Wow, look how he's carving that beef roast; sure you're not a French chef in disguise, Dad?"

"Neat maneuver, Pop! You're the best Chevrolet driver in town, bar none."

Idea #2. *The hyperbole of honor.*

In most happy homes there's a great deal of blithe banter. The give and take of teasing is a part of treasured affection and comradeship. Sometimes, as we've just been noticing, the jokes can become dirks and daggers of scorn, and Dad's morale bleeds. (Nicks and bleeding can happen to any person in any group, of course. But it's your father we're thinking about just now. And we need to remember that tremors can come to the health of a society when fathers bleed.)

Instead of the teasing that cuts him down, how about experimenting with the humor that elevates?

Telephone rings. "Is Mr. Fred Doe in?" asks an unknown voice.

You grin, hold out the receiver, pretend a medieval knight's intonation. "His majesty King Frederick is desired."

You pick up the keys for a trip to the filling station. "And does the President of this Doe corporation also desire the oil to be changed in the Doe limousine?"

Idea #3. In many optional matters consult his opinions freely and watch his wishes attentively.

"Which football game do *you* want to watch this afternoon, Dad?"

"No, thanks, Ted. Yeah, I was thinking about tennis, but Dad wants a hand in trimming the hedges tonight. . . ."

"Since each of us has a different nomination, let's make Daddy decide. Will the Dairy Queen or Kentucky Fried or the Chinese place be more pleasing to Your Royal Highness?"

Yes, Mom's wishes are important too, and sometimes she is appropriately "queen for a day." But for steady fare it's often good when other family members can practice the aphorism that "Daddy knows best."

Once when I was a very young staff member at what was then Seattle Pacific College, I spent a summer as the speaker (and chaperone for the pianist) with a traveling male quartet. The whole group was near my own age bracket, and each musician had practical wisdoms beyond mine, but the summer went better than it might have, I truly believe, because the S.P.C. music director gave us a Dutch-uncle talk before we left. "In any group," he said firmly, "somebody must make the final decisions. You talk things over, but somebody must decide. In this group Dr. McAllaster is to make the decisions. Okay? Is that clear?"

In a thousand situations within any home someone must decide. As you can pitch the decisions toward your father and nudge others in the family to do the same, you will increasingly honor him.

Idea #4. *Redirect the spotlights.* Sometimes the weapon Mother has been putting into her Edward's hands, unwittingly or well aware, is to ignore or downgrade Dad's employment and his achievements. Are you an Edward of that sort? If you pause to think of it, does Dad really seem to exist for her only at home? Does what he does to acquire a paycheck really interest her less than a little?

Obviously what is ideal in one home might be awkward in another, and some men find it much more restorative to their spirits to leave office topics at the office. Yet many a man greatly needs—and does not get—his family's warm and sympathetic and admiring interest in his workaday world.

Can you experiment with intelligent, informed questions?

Whatever he does—crops, sales, architecture, law, garbage collecting, welding—can you do it with him vicariously? Can you give him a worthy audience?

Especially can you enable him to let the whole family rejoice with him when his rejoicings come? A new account landed, a field of soybeans harvested, a customer overtly pleased. Can it become easier and easier to suggest, "Hey, *that* calls for a celebration, Father! Mom, why don't we all go down to Baskin-Robbins to salute the occasion?" (Or would popping corn be your kind of celebration? Or making tacos? Or lettering humorous certificates on parchment, "BE IT KNOWN UNTO ALL MEN BY THESE PRESENTS. . . . ")

As I ask you those questions, Edward, I think of a home I visited. Mr. Blank was pretty widely known across America for his career in the visual arts, but as I think back to living room and dining room, to the kitchen and to the master bedroom where I left a coat, I cannot recall seeing even one snapshot of one work he had produced. Dinner conversation: did we talk about any of his new plans or his former commissions? I can't recall that we did. His extroverted, talkative family could, I think, have done him daily honor by question and comment and exclamation.

Mrs. Blank liked her job more than she respected his, it seemed. Certainly the walls of their home all said that she did. (And her son's sword dropped blood, dropped blood, dropped blood.)

Idea #5. *Traditions, traditions.*

Any home builds its little traditions, its inside jokes, its recurrent episodes, with deepening layers of meaning. Sometimes the habits develop without planning. Sometimes they are pain-induced and pain-producing habits at the intersection of Mom's anger and Dad's resentment.

Are there some little traditions you can begin or continue that will honor a mortal father while you have the chance?

Memory flicks. I'm eight years old again. My sister and I are standing near the coal-burning cookstove with breakfast-hungry eyes on a plate of pancakes Mother has been baking. A big plate, to serve six siblings and two parents. One of us starts counting and doing a sum in division. "Three apiece, and five for Daddy," she reports. A practical little tradition that my canny mother had instigated and all of us adhered to: Daddy gets the extra in any dividing. Our hero. Our muscle-man. Our Daddy.

Another farmhouse tradition of that era: no noise of dishes now if Daddy needs a noontime nap. (Sometimes out in the summer fields by four A.M., he often did need one.)

What little traditions for you?

The triumphal march from *Aïda* in the stereo whenever Dad comes back from a business trip? For a long, hard trip inflated party ballons and crepe paper streamers to greet him?

Doughnuts and cider each year on the anniversary of his ordination?

A backyard barbecue in his honor when his bowling team wins?

Idea #6. *Talk things over.*

Whatever your age, whatever the precariousness or essential closeness of the sutures between Mom and Dad and you, would it be helpful now and then to say candidly, calmly, honestly, "Look, Mom, I think that . . . "?

Would it be good to talk bluntly with your siblings about the specific ways wherein one parent is making it hard and harder for you to honor another parent?

Would it be good to have an occasional family council with the others about how you are and are not keeping in step with the Sinai command?

Idea #7. *Don't talk it over.*

A time for everything under the sun, said the ancient Proverbs. There is a time to confide, to discuss; there is also a time to put finger to lip and keep silent.

If yours is a mother who speaks anger and tirades against your father, you may need again and again to say quietly, "Mother, I shouldn't be hearing this." You may need to urge, "Look, save *that* to tell to the pastor when you see him tomorrow afternoon." You may need to let her know with deep love that you share her pain but you have a double loyalty that must put stoppers in your ears.

Sometimes her need to confide will be greater than her wisdom about confiding. Can you help her to be wise? A friend of mine mentioned to me how a widow well past eighty reminisced to her of the fifty-years-ago inclinations to leave her husband. It was better that the widow told my outsider friend, I'm sure, rather than telling her now middle-aged son. The need to confide was perhaps inexplicable; to a son, it might have been also irreparable, a stain upon a father's memory. If the widow were to start reminiscing in such veins to her son, I would hope he could quickly and gently divert her to other recollections.

Idea #8. *Try to understand subordinate causes.*

You're not a marriage counselor, Edward, and you shouldn't try to become one. But sometimes a new insight can wonderfully strengthen your compassion, and it may strengthen your hands when you are, willy-nilly, an intermediary.

Right now I'm thinking about the Kelly family. (We'll call them Kelly.) When I knew them I was recurrently startled-astounded at Tom Kelly's surly language to his wife, his dark angers, his vicious looks flung at her. Young Sam Kelly might easily have been provoked to say on any day during that era, "Dad, I love Mother, and the way you treat her is causing me to hate you," or he might have been goaded to violent action. Instead, so far as I observed, he maintained a surprising teen-age equanimity. As I have thought about the Kellys since I last saw them, I have realized that Tom's surliness was rooted, more than I then knew, in the dreadfully precarious balance of his business. Half a step from bankruptcy and half wild with financial uncertainties, he spoke from within dark desperations. And Sam had helped his father at work enough to have some reading on the torments Tom was experiencing and to be forbearing.

A friend of mine has written some powerful poetry about his early and lingering hatred for his now-long-dead father. In a letter to me my friend commented poignantly, "It used to be when I looked at a picture of him, I saw strength and hardness. Now I see wistfulness and a bewildered inability to cope with the world, most of all to cope with human realities."

If you can see clearly now, Edward, while your father is yet with you . . . I can't tell you how earnestly I wish clarity of vision for you!

It won't always be possible for you to know *why* your mother is handing you a sword. If you can come to understand, it may help you to keep sheathing sword after sword after sword!

Idea #9. *To pray for them both!*

No topic in this whole world is too small to pray about—nor too large. The emotional balance in a family is always a right-sized topic for prayer. Always, always, always.

Where prayer—deep, yearning, prevailing prayer, prayer in the name of our Lord Christ—will lead, no one can say.

It isn't up to you to assess blame, to tell God whom to forgive or for what. He knows whether and where "fault" becomes "sin," whether and where "temperament" means "guilt" in his sight. You don't need to know. He is utter love. He loves both the parents you yearn to honor, and he loves you as you stand between them. Blessings, blessings to you!

Another flick of memory, and I'm back in a farmhouse in western Kansas. We always knelt for family prayer after breakfast; that tradition was almost as certain as sunrise. One phrase my mother often used lodged in my grade-school brain: "And help us to be to each other as we should." Although I did not begin to comprehend the immense subtleties of lives interweaving with other lives inside a family unit, I valued her prayer; I value it still. And I hand it to you for your using: " . . . to be to each other as we should."

16

WHAT WOULD IT MEAN FOR CRAIG?

Recently in using a notebook of my poems I noticed a penciled comment on the back of a page reminding me that when it was new the poem was shared with Craig. Since I saw the notation, my thoughts have been echoing "Craig, Craig, Craig" very persistently.

He's past twenty-five now. He's probably one of the more gifted persons I've had the good pleasure of conferring with in the past ten years. I haven't seen him for quite a while, but all the cues and clues one catches would say Craig is now living a rather fragmented life, a regrettably aimless life. While his brilliant mind and his decisions drift with the currents, his parents are geographically and emotionally many miles away from him—or he from them. He carries inside himself both mild amiability and deep animosity toward them, especially toward his father.

Whimsical "what if" thoughts have been spinning in my mind. What if some fantasy experiences would come to Craig (from Narnia, or from Madeleine L'Engle's settings, or from "Twilight Zone," or from Scrooge) for the next year or so? What if he would see ads dissolving away on billboards, with "Honor your father" emblazoned instead? What if by night he would dream recurrently of standing before a tribunal with a judge instructing him to Honor, and to Honor, and to Honor? What if faerie voices would keep singing arias of "Honor" whenever he hears guitars or violins or trumpets on his stereo and at all the concerts?

And then what if he would start experimenting with ways to obey the instruction of the billboards and the judges and the faerie voices? In a year's time what could it mean in Craig's life? What might he try?

The questions are worth speculating about beyond the level of fantasy and amusement. Insofar as I know Craig and his family, I am quite sure that many of the "might happen" items in his life would parallel "might happen" items in the lives of many, many other young people. There's only one Craig Newsome—as I'll call him—but yet there are thousands of him.

Will you let me make some guesses about Craig? Will you check the ones that have your name implicit in them also?

* * *

—Some morning soon Craig will waken and watch Linda until she, too, is awake. Then he will tell her with finality that she is a sweet kid and all that, but if she still isn't interested in marriage, one of them will just have to move. "We've kept saying that things are fine while we are being honest with each other and that nobody is getting hurt, but it's mud on our parents' reputations, and we know it."

—Craig may not change jobs, or he may. (He knows Judge Newsome isn't especially proud to have him pumping gas, but the career decisions he will have to work through on his own.) He will find himself talking more about his dad to the other employees. He may quote some of the Judge's ideas on integrity, and he may grin about childhood's first lessons on windshields while he whistles and cleans the latest windshield to arrive.

—One of these days Craig's mind will hear Judge Newsome saying grace at the table, or see the Newsomes being seated in the family pew at church. Craig will think, and wonder, and pick up a newspaper to see when church services begin in his town. Later, he will be angry and tense and unwilling when he pushes open a swinging oak door to a narthex, but he will also be glad. In their honor.

—The studio photo of Dad that Mom gave him last Christmas will come out of his footlocker and find a place on his dresser. He will often scrutinize those eyebrows, that mouth, and put quizzical inquiries to them.

—He will determine to get to know Judge Newsome as a person, as a human being. Ever since the shouting matches and ultimatums when Craig was in high school, there has been distance and uneasy truce. "Maybe everybody else in town liked Dad better than I did," he admits. "Than I do. You always assume you *know* your own family, but I don't think I do. Not really. Will he let me? When I go home, I'll take him out to lunch and give it a try. Hey. Have I *ever* eaten a meal with Dad, just the two of us?"

—He will stop at the post office for a supply of postcards and of stamps to use on scenic view cards. He will send news items about his canoe trips, his bowling scores. Sometimes he'll be picking up the telephone to tell a plan, to convey a small tiding. To honor them with his personal news, even when it is tiny. (Not that he will be moving into a retrogressive dependence; he won't try to become ten again, but his present mature self will become more visible, more sharing.)

—Sometime, amused, he will salute Dad's preferences, even in Dad's absence.

To order liver and onions as he thinks about how much Dad would enjoy sharing that meal. To watch a *National Geographic* special on TV and think about how Dad would be commenting on it. To turn on a little more volume in cheering basketball skills that Dad would applaud. (I am not suggesting, though, that Craig will now modify all his hobbies and recreations to match with Judge Newsome's. He may not modify any. He and his father are very different in temperament, in proclivities, in what they really enjoy.)

—He will develop more of his Craig-liness, his own skills, his potential. He's the kind of person who as a college freshman could mutter angrily, "I'm *sick* of hearing about my *potential*"—but anyone would say the potential is there, far beyond what is now being realized.

What a birthday gift it would be for his father if Craig could write home to say that he is taking some night classes in math at the local community college, or that he is learning Italian by cassettes and correspondence, or that he has joined an amateur drama club! (A gift, in any case; a brighter, more jubilantly received gift if Craig would say outright, "And this project is for *you*, Dad. Wish me luck.")

—He will find a new release from the old resentments, from all the old scars.

They're there. The teen years were often shrill and harsh and angry. But as Craig thinks "Honor, Honor, Honor" about fifty times a day in response to Narnia or dissolving billboards, he will find scars healing and changing and blending and diminishing. The remembering will be different.

Sometimes little laughters may help the healing. Maybe a dime store photo of Craig just after a haircut, sent with a light-hearted comment, since Craig's ponytail era was one of such bitter friction. (I'm thinking right now of a tall young man who came into a hospital room I was visiting three days ago and said jovially, "Hey, Mom, I got a haircut! See?" His pleasure, and hers, were pleasant to watch; probably he was a better tonic than any medicine dispensed that day.)

—The expressed appreciations. The expressed affections. I

haven't seen the Newsomes together enough to be totally sure of anything, but my guess would certainly be that Craig has found words of endearment very, very hard to speak aloud, that even a "Hey, thanks" usually sticks to his tonsil scars rather than being spoken. In a year's time he could do a lot of practicing—a lot of catching up on the "Hey, thanks" expressions that probably go back to the era of his tricycles and his rompers.

* * *

Whatever specific experiments Craig tries, I'm deeply convinced that he will actually be experimenting toward his own deep happiness. More than he thinks or dreams right now, the harsh homeward feelings are a key log in the tangled log jam of his life. (Have you read Ralph Connor's novels or other accounts of logging operations on American and Canadian rivers? You will remember how one log, straightened around, lets many others float more freely.)

"I like me as I am," Craig might sputter or grin if pointed questions were put to him today. But he will like the newer-model Craig a great deal more. I'm convinced of that—for the real-life Craig with whom I shared a poem once and for all the real-life Craigs everywhere.

17

ADDRESS UNKNOWN

While I was skimming the back page of a newspaper two nights ago, one sentence in a glanced-through obituary left me reeling. Millicent Turner had died—I fictionize the names—and the column of type recited the list of her relatives: "Survivors include two daughters, Mary Galbraith of Springfield and Winifred Wilson of Rochester; son, Robert, address unknown; eleven grandchildren. . . . "

Address unknown.

Son, Robert, address unknown.

Did he leave home during the hippie exodus of the 'sixties? Has he been moving from job to job on the west coast? Is he living somewhere in Chicago's grimier warrens of smudgy apartments?

Address unknown.

Did he walk out after a raging quarrel? Or after ten thousand little frictions? Did he enlist in the Marines and decide not to come home again? Did the Turners issue ultimatums he couldn't accept? Did he issue ultimatums they couldn't accept?

Now his mother is dead, and no one has known how to tell him about her funeral.

Address unknown.

The emotion of it resonates through me like bells in a carillon. Robert Turner and how many thousands more like him out across America? Contact has been broken and young people out there beyond the horizon want it to stay broken. Utterly, totally, finally broken.

I didn't know Robert Turner, but I do know Hal. His face has been haunting me since I noticed it several weeks ago when I was checking something in a several-years-ago college yearbook. Hal: winsome, brilliant, idealistic, witty. Hal: suddenly AWOL from his family a year or two after his graduation. Hal. Silences. Anger. Silences. Anger. Address unknown.

The missing person isn't new to American society nor to the present decade. The frontiers were partially settled—American frontiers, Canadian frontiers, Australian frontiers—by young men who wanted desperately to find a new start, to become incognito, to avoid all recognition from post offices and telegraph offices. But that doesn't make the strain and pain and agony any less for the fractured families of now, does it?

Recently (as I've thought and thought about Hal) a ballad from early in this century has kept humming in my head. My mother used to sing its plaintive cadences during housework:

Has anybody here seen Kelly?
K—E—double L—Y,
Kelly, from the Emerald Isle?
Sure, his hair is red, and eyes are blue.
Yes, he is Irish through and through—
Kelly with the green necktie.

Kelly was missing somewhere in an older New York City, and somebody was looking for him eagerly, plaintively, up and down all the avenues. Kelly represented a great many others back at the turn of the century, and he represents a great many others now. This evening.
Kelly.
Hal.
Robert Turner.
No known address.

* * *

Are you one of that fraternity?

If you are, it really doesn't matter to you whether a million others have preceded you in wrenching loose from home ties. Your private drama is your own; the only life you'll ever live is this one, now. As I say that, a strong, strong cry is fairly jolted from me, and I feel like pleading (or yelling) in campus parlance: Don't blow it, this one life of yours!

Whatever has happened up to now, you have this now. Don't blow it. Please don't blow it!

Out there wherever you are, address unknown: may I put a few thoughts into your muscled fingers?

First: whatever you have told yourself (morning, noon, and night, and between times), it *does* make a difference to the rest of the world that you are out of touch with your home base. Your life is *not* just your own life to enjoy or to waste or to fling away. You are one part of a big, big network linked and interlinked and cross-linked in more ways than you can possibly know. Your separation from a family deadens landscapes, stultifies human contacts, handicaps the very angels. Just as a tiny cinder in your eye can make your whole body uncomfortable and dismayed and frustrated, so your absence stings an entire body-of-us-all.

* * *

Secondly. Somebody cares about the episodes and attitudes—whatever they were—that caused you to hitchhike to Los Angeles, or to take a job with migrant wheat harvesters, or to settle at a commune in Oregon, or whatever you did to become an "address unknown." (Whatever, whatever, whatever!) Somebody cares about your moods now. Somebody cares about *you*.

Somebody cares.

Probably your parents care about a thousand times more than you thought they would.

Your siblings.

Your neighbors.

Your friends.

Friends of your friends.

More than you know, more than you would have guessed, they care.

If you were to tap at your parents' back door this very evening, would a whole neighborhood be electric with gladness by midnight? Would gladdened telephone calls be sending bright sparks to other towns, to other states? People probably care, more than you have known that they care.

And I care.

Robert, Hal, Kelly: I care. While there is a bitterness of spirit between two persons on this earth, an alienation, a dark and dreadful silence, I care.

And because I care so desperately, I am very sure there are others near you, or about to be near you, who are ready to care also.

A pastor who would talk with you? A friend who is a for-real and undeniable friend, not merely a good-time Mick? A neighbor? A relative? Somebody at work who knows more than the how-to of the daily tasks—who knows about human personalities and how they can maim or heal each other?

In the midst of all the other carings, there is One who enables any other caring to happen, whenever it does. He is God your Maker—and your utter Friend, whether you have ever yet recognized him as your Friend or not. He knew about it when you and your parents first said strained and bitter words to each other. He knew when you decided you could not bear any more of any more, and he knew exactly why you felt that way. He knows every quivering aspiration you have ever felt toward self-realization, toward a different identity, toward newness of being.

He knows, too, what good things can happen next if you let him call the signals. He knows, and he cares.

A further observation, while I think about a letter that came just a few weeks ago from the father of a present-day "K-E-double L-Y." Some pretty intense emotions permeated all his paragraphs, believe me.

It is not right—it cannot be right—for one human being to cause another human being as much suffering as you are causing to your father.

Do you think of your dad only as the stern man whose reproofs you urgently needed to escape? Maybe he was stern; he is also affection, and yearning, and pain. His emotions, day by day, while you are living out there in "address unknown," are like blisters and cactus needles and broken bones and migraines.

Are you gentle toward horses and dogs, toward furred and flying creatures? Fathers, too, are an endangered species on this big blue marble we call earth; fathers too need steady, responsible affection—and need it more than dogs or horses can.

"His fault," do you mutter? But nothing is ever totally anyone's fault, not on this human earth. And now, Address Unknown, the next move is up to *you*.

* * *

For your own completeness, now, you need to make a move toward him.

You are, in part, the sum of many, many relationships. With one crucial relationship snuffed out and ignored, a part of *you* is absent. Have you ever slangily mocked at someone who wasn't "all there"? While you are out of touch with the flesh that gave you flesh, with the lives that gave you life, you aren't "all there." You cannot be. (You, Robert Turner. You, Hal. You, Kelly. You, all of you who have walked out, hitch-hiked off, run away, "split the scene" in any fashion whatsoever.)

You're like one of those old Greek or Roman statues one sees in the museums: an arm broken off, an ear chipped away, a nose blunted. But now with the renewal of filial relationships the broken statuary can grow new pieces in ways that will surprise you.

* * *

Have you realized that your father, too, is sentenced to a fragmentary existence while you're out of his life?

No matter if you have half a dozen siblings—or a dozen, like a woman I heard from just yesterday; your father's life is bound up with *your* life. Without *you* he is not fully himself and cannot be.

In times past has it given you a vindictive and vengeful gladness to know that your absence was slicing off some of your father's very selfhood? As you are becoming more of a man and putting away childish things, can you outgrow that kind of petty savagery? Can you loyally hand to your father the enablement to be fully himself?

In so doing you are moving with the very grain of the universe instead of against it, you know. Water is designed to flow downhill; heat rises; gravity pulls ripened apples earthward; flames give off heat. That's their nature. Fish swim—that's their nature. Birds soar and glide—that's their nature. To give honor to parents is, similarly, built into the very nature things. We are meant to work that way, and the delicate machinery of human personality grinds and tears when we violate such a primal principle.

* * *

Another observation, another principle: what *has* been does not limit nor preclude what is yet to be.

Suppose you've been "address unknown" for five years. You've made a new identity for yourself, found new associates, affirmed new lifestyles. You can't imagine a renewal of the old-home identity. You can't imagine, either, a peaceful coexistence with the parents you disowned.

But we live in a world of tomorrows, not just of yesterdays. Not even primarily of yesterdays. The yet-to-be is worth agonizingly great efforts.

Dead relationships can come to life again. They really can. They won't be a replica of what used to be; you'll never be eight again, nor ten, nor twelve. But there can be a splendid, radiant newness. C. S. Lewis wrote that the one prayer that is certainly wrong to pray is an "encore" prayer. To ask to have things become again just as they were before you flexed your leg muscles and hiked away is an unworthy "encore" prayer. But there can be a newness that is new and right and beautiful and restored.

It is Easter night as I write these paragraphs. The white trumpets of an Easter lily are filling this room with fragrance. "Tombs can open," they affirm. Because one gritty-hard actual tombstone was flung aside, once, over there in ancient Israel, all sorts of other stones can be flung aside. Stones of misunderstanding, anger, resentment, filial rebellions. Stones of separation. Stones of alienation.

Outdoors today I reveled in the clean fresh newness of April landscapes. White dogwood petals shower through the incredible green of April-new foliage all across this town.

For you, too, for the barren wintry landscapes inside your frozen emotions, an Easter is waiting.

* * *

"Address unknown"? In alumni files and on magazine rosters that label may need to have a usefulness. Within a family it should never, never, never need to be used. If emotionally it stands written on all your T-shirts, it's time for you to run (Don't walk; run!) to the nearest telephone and dial a long-familiar number.

* * *

Have you been *hearing* me, Robert Turner? Have you *heard* me, Hal?

I could wish that neon billboards would encircle you hourly, blazoning and persuading, "Honor your father. . . . " I could wish you would hear Sinai thunders in the rumble of trains or the throb of auto motors. I could wish for you a great shipment of new courage, of gentleness, of patience. I could wish . . . I could wish. . . .

But it's not now a time for my wishing; it's a time for your acting.

It's your move now. Tonight and tomorrow and on through all the tomorrows. A first contact won't solve everything, but the renewals won't come without a first contact, and you're the one to make it.

Will you let your address be known again? Will you do it soon?

* * *

Now a week of my life has gone by. And of yours. Different trumpets on the Easter lily are showering out their white perfumes. At 2:00 A.M., I'm suddenly wakeful and yearning toward the Hals of America.

My mother telephoned me earlier tonight during the lovely long spring twilight, and it was a gentle, happy conversation. "Nothing special on my mind," she assured me. "I just wanted to hear your voice." She heard it only a few days ago, she hears it often, but she had a hungering need to hear it tonight. Now I glance over at the little white gadget that brought her voice to me, that took my voice to her, and I think about Hal, about all the Hals whose voices have not been heard by more yearning parental ears for weeks, for months, for accruing dreadful years. As I turn back to my 2:00 A.M. pillow, I'll be sending some prayer-telegrams out toward places where other telegrams cannot now be sent: "WRITE, OR WIRE, OR CALL, HAL. NOW. IT'S URGENT. YOU'RE NEEDED."

Now, while you still can.

With an odd poignant resignation in her voice a woman I know said once she suddenly realized there is no person in the world to whom she is the most important person in the world. Father: deceased. Mother: deceased. All her other human ties: more tenuous, or at an end, or not yet begun.

Maybe, Hal, you're "most important" to several persons in your now-world, but you're still achingly "most important" to the two human beings who gave you life, and for you "deceased" does not stand written across their names. Not yet. Not now, tonight. If there were a car accident tomorrow or a coronary before dawn comes, potentialities would change.

Here beside me the alarm clock ticks, ticks, ticks, ticks while I turn to fluff a pillow. Your life is ticking away, too, Hal. And their lives, made daily more meager by your silences. Whatever—*whatever* —the barriers have been, will you let love and honor impel you into action, Hal? (You, every Hal in America!) Now. Today.

18

WHEN YOU TELL GOD ABOUT HIM . . .

Yesterday at a potluck dinner I was seated with an engineer from the McDonnell-Douglas Company in St. Louis and his gracious wife. While we munched, Mr. Engineer told the rest of us with some excitement about his perspective on what computers are doing for us, could do for us, will do for us.

His eager enthusiasm is wryly in my thoughts this morning, making some odd connections any engineer would hardly predict. Datum 1: A while ago I heard bells ringing in the dim distance summoning people to early prayer in a local brick building with a tall up-pointing spire. Datum 2: Praying voices in the mode of ancient Gregorian chant are now filling this room with softly sung cadences. Datum 3: Since long before dawn today I have been thinking about *you*. You and your father. The disharmonies. The tensions. The yearnings.

Putting those pieces of new data together in the computer housed inside my skull—along with all that's already in the memory bank there —brings a new printout.

It's a question I am to set before you. When you pray about him, how do you pray? What do you ask or say or beg when you tell God about your father?

Let's keep the computer image for a moment.

If a precise and detailed printout could be secured of every prayer for him that has traversed your mind within the past six months, what would we read on the big perforated pages? Not just formal prayers. Not just prayers spoken aloud or verbalized when you were kneeling in a church or kneeling beside a chair in your bedroom. Real prayer may also include the incoherent unspoken groan ("O God, O God, O God") and the lambent silent yearnings that flicker and burn, flicker and burn inside you.

Lacking the visual evidence of a computer printout, would you think about it? What does memory suggest?

Sometimes has there been a baffled tendency to push Dad out of your conscious prayers because you simply didn't know how to pray or what to pray? As I pose that inquiry, I think quickly of the hesitant perplexity and frustration I saw on Willy's earnest freckled countenance one time while he shared some deep-level emotions. When Willy discovered Christianity through Campus Crusade at a university, he wanted everyone, and especially his family, to share his new joy. Most especially his father, whom he loved dearly. He prayed fervently for his father. Time went on, and Dad's resistance to Willy's new faith was flinty firm. Still he prayed. Then came Dad's divorce, the disintegration of human-level relationships, increasing alienation. "I just don't know *how* to pray for him now," Willy confessed. "My faith isn't very strong, I guess. He seems so remote, in every way. . . . "

Only baffled groping uncertain prayers would be on Willy's printout then.

On Carl's maybe even less. Carl has such bitter feeling, if my perceptions have been accurate, that he keeps training himself to repress almost all the father-recollections and father-allusions. If he makes prayer lists now, his father would probably rank somewhere after the newsboy, the streetcar conductor, and his office janitor. In impromptu prayers Carl's mind would probably leapfrog from Mom to nephews to former roommates to missionaries and carefully bounce right across Dad.

Wayne. I can almost see Wayne's cynical grin and the decisive twitch of his pony tail. "Count me out, Dr. Mac. You know I don't pray no prayers about nothin', and certainly not about *him*." I grin back but in a different key. Not yet, Wayne, not yet. Your life isn't over yet, thank God.

Dave?

Dave would probably look sheepish and confess that his prayers have centered on his exams, his employment, and his applications for grad school. Not many real prayers for anyone else. Certainly not many real prayers about Dad. Oh, he breathes little blessings as he did when he was six or seven: "Bless Mom, bless Dad, bless Kim and Kate and Georgie." But the blessings don't carry much real impact inside him or beyond him.

Scott?

"Well, I pray for him," Scott might murmur, "but mostly, I guess, when I feel rotten after we've had a big hassle over my grades or the car or something, and I don't like to be such a mess inside, and I ask God to change Dad, someway or another, so he won't be so hard to get along with. Am I a creep to pray that way?"

Nobody is a creep who prays earnestly about whatever troubles him, Scott. Maybe those prayers will lead you to some deeper, broader prayers.

"Like what?" he frowns. "Like what?"

Long pause.

I take a deep breath or two and hesitate. You will each have to hew your own path, I say slowly. Every human being has to work out his own salvation with fear and trembling, as St. Paul admonished. But I am eager to share something from Catherine Marshall that I believe can speak to your situation. In her book *Adventures in Prayer* Catherine Marshall has a chapter called "The Prayer of Joyous Blessing." May I hope you will look it up soon and read it about forty times?

As she describes it, this is a sharply focused prayer—not a "bless everyone everywhere" generalization, but a prayer that encircles one person. It is not an evaluating prayer asking blessing upon someone who deserves or doesn't deserve. It is not an accusatory prayer that specifies someone's flaws and tells God what to change in the someone. Rather, letting God's love and joy flow through you, the joyous blessing prayer asks God to rain his blessings—whether spiritual or physical or material—on the one for whom we pray and leaves all outcomes trustingly to him.

Would you be willing to experiment, valiantly and earnestly, with precisely that kind of prayer for your father? "Give him, O God, your blessings for this day" could be a casual litany, but I don't mean that. From the centermost marrow of your bones, can you implore blessing and blessing and blessing? In homely metaphor, can you become like a garden hose that conveys rotating sprays of moisture from the reservoir to parched lawn grasses?

I am glad Catherine Marshall stresses leaving all the outcomes to God in the "joyous blessing" prayer. At other times precise intercessions are right and good, but when "I don't even know how to pray for him!" is our plight, there can be a beautiful and holy relaxation in the trustful "bless" that does not specify a "Give."

In his great book entitled simply *Prayer* George Buttrick offers the suggestion that no situation stays the same when it is a prayed-about situation. His voice would join Catherine Marshall's—and mine- in inviting you to the prayer of joyous blessing.

Perhaps you would find it helpful (useful? exhilarating?) to try a very specific laboratory experience in the school of prayer. Might it be a good thing to get a little spiral notebook and record when and where and what you pray about your father for, say, the next six months? You could enter some blessing verses that now seem to have his name written into them. You could also confess before our loving Lord in cryptogram or written words your own day-by-day new filial needs—the times of anger that engulf you, the frictions that dismay you.

Six months from now the little notebook could be a new kind of printout that the angels themselves will read with deep interest as they look over your mortal shoulders.

Whether you ever write down a prayer or not, do have in mind that "Dad-and-me" is never, never a total unit among human equations. Whether you have recognized the other component or not, "Dad-and-God-and-me" is always written into the nature of things. To talk with Dad about God is not always possible; to talk with God about Dad is always an open opportunity.

What will immortal computers print out from your praying about your father during these next six months?

19

TO KEEP ON HOPING

According to one of our familiar proverbs, "Hope springs eternal in the human breast." Thank God that it does! All of us need the courage of our optimisms, the renewal of spirit that comes from ever-new sustaining hopes.

Yet hopes need realism, too, or they can turn into tools that gash us while we try to wield them. Specifically, the conscious and sub-conscious hopes you cherish about a bettering of your relationship with your father can, long-term, be very important in your morale, your self-concepts, your usefulness to the world.

There are various angles to consider. Some of the angles will come into view, I think, if I talk with you a little about George and Tom, two brothers I know moderately well. Their parental home came apart when the boys were both in their teens, and from other sources I am well aware that the divorce was a dismal and bitter one. Since the divorce George has coped very well, completing college with high honors and going on to an excellent job. Everywhere he has gone he has made warm friendships and been involved in satisfying, wholesome activities. Tom, in contrast, has floundered and floundered and floundered. Drugs. Alcohol. Problems with jobs.

Obviously many factors have been at work. Their mother would probably have told us that they differed in all sorts of ways when they were two or four or seven. But one crucial and identifiable difference more recently has seemed to be right at this point of realism in their hopes. ("Seemed," I'm saying carefully; I'm neither clairvoyant nor omniscient.) Tom has seemed to keep hoping, probably more than he knows, that the volcano of parental divorce will be reversed, like a movie running backwards; that the lava will flow back into the earth, and Dad will be married to Mom again. More consciously, he keeps hoping that Dad will be more affectionate, more reliable, more pres-ent to Tom's needs than he ever is. Result: daily disillusionment; in-creasing bitterness and anger.

George, on the other hand, seems to have squared his sturdy shoulders and recognized that he must make his own decisions and successes without hoping for much of a hand from home. When I asked him once about parental approval of some complex vacation plans he had made, George shrugged a little. "I've been pretty much on my own since I was in junior high," he told me. When he commented a little on a faculty home where he had often been entertained, he said quietly (and quite without rancor) that it was "sort of my home, insofar as I have a home."

George and Tom would illustrate a principle, then, that will apply in a great many situations: high and unreasoning hopes can bring constant pain, realistically lowered hopes can mean increased contentment.

Some of the mail I've been receiving illustrates some other principles. Acrid words from Dennis would show that often one simply does not know what to hope for. Praying for Dad now is like praying for a stranger, Dennis says. The new stepmother does not welcome him, his father does not care to see him, an infant half-sister increases the sense of utter alienation. What hope has he, and for what?

A note from Susan of quite another sort. She had gone to see her father (whom she had earlier assumed to be dead) after twenty years of separation, and there has been a "precious reconciliation," a fulfillment of her hopes beyond what she had expected.

A letter from Walt. His father, in another city, was about to have major surgery, and Walt telephoned to express his concern. "And he told me he loves me," Walt writes gladly. "I wanted so much to hear him say he loves me, and he did!"

As we weave those letters into our thinking along with all the other threads already on the looms of thought, can we see some of the following patterns emerging?

—It is not useful to hope for a restoration of the past. In the wording of Thomas Wolfe's novel title, we simply can't go home again. Our little Edens are behind us, as well as the primeval Eden. Can we helpfully recognize that some of our frustration and bitter anger flows out from hidden and subconscious and unreal hopes for what can never be again?

—To hope that *another person* will change toward us may not be fruitful; to hope that *we* can change in our ability to respond to that person may be very fruitful.

Dennis: you can hope and pray for God's great love within your life. More than he would ever admit right now, your father needs your human love. Not an iffy kind of love ("If he would apologize to me," "if he and Alice would treat me the way I deserve") but encompassing, unconditional love.

You can hope and pray that Grace will touch every contact you have with him. That you will manifest the attitudes that God will give you.

To illustrate in tiny measure what I'm thinking about here: I once had an acquaintance who often battered my spirits by her overwhelming egotism. Any conversation with her would move within seconds to recitals of her illnesses or her troubles or her achievements or her cat's achievements or her anything. When I sputtered inwardly and wished she would change the habits of her self-centered preoccupations, I was like someone throwing sand against the wind. When I could face the realization that she was not likely to change but I could respond either Gracelessly or Gracefully, things went better! Can you put less hope in his changing and more hope in your loving, Dennis?

It is always good to hope for another person's Christian renewal. Just how you pray will need care. "I hope he will become a better Christian soon so he will be nicer to me" would be more of a selfish impulse than a real prayer. But you can hope most earnestly and most rightly that God will shower him with blessings.

—To keep hoping for new measures of openness and affection and peace is certainly good. Walt has hoped, and hoped, and hoped, and now his hopes have seen fruition. If he had let himself become blasé and uncaring, if he had dismissed his hopes, he would not have heard the now-cherished words of affection.

—To take specific action may be necessary and helpful in fulfilling your hopes. Susan made a trip. She went to her long-alienated father. It took an effort, a strenuous one emotionally and otherwise, but she went. Similarly, Walt picked up the telephone before his father's surgery; he took an initiative. He made his affection and concern known audibly at a crucial time.

One of my creative colleagues, Dr. James Reinhard, has spoken in sermons and chapel talks of our need to "tangibilicate" our beliefs, to make them tangible. To show them in ways that can be heard, smelled, seen, touched, tasted. Walt has "tangibilicated" his hopes in placing a telephone call that could be heard. Hopes that stay inside you may not cause much to happen. Hopes expressed in ways that can be smelled and touched and tasted may eventually have splendid and beautiful outcomes.

St. Paul was not writing casually when he told the Corinthians that hope "abideth." It is a wonderfully important ingredient in our human lives. For each of us struggling mortals, and certainly not least for each who struggles against his filial estrangements, hope "abideth." It abides, as Paul expressed it, within a team: "And now abideth faith, hope, charity." For us, as for the ancient Corinthians, hope can surely "abide" when we keep it within that wonderful team. Toward unreconciled fathers as in all other concerns we need the further benediction of Brother Paul's reminder: the strong, firm, selfless love that early translations called "charity" is indeed the greatest.

May your hopes be realistic, energetic, durable, sustaining. Wherever it's possible, hope on, hope on!

20

DURING A TWILIGHT

Sunday evening. Twilight. Outside my room a sleepy robin chweeters and chweeters. Inside my room thoughts about a young man in Texas who has written me about his bitter feelings toward his father. (Since it isn't actually Texas, I'll say Texas.) He's so much on my mind I almost pick up the telephone, but I don't know what number would reach him tonight.

I think and ponder and wonder. I wonder if Jack has moved several meters closer to God on this worship day, and if so I wonder how his Dadward responses were changed by his deeper and more earnest Godward responses.

Sometimes to obey God in new ways means new alienations. I pick up my much-thumbed oldest Bible and leaf to Matthew 10: "Think not that I am come to send peace on earth: I came not to send peace, but a sword. For I am come to set a man at variance against his father. . . . " It stabs deeply (while I think about Jack) to notice that the relationship our Lord named first of all—presumably the deepest, most primal, most difficult to sever of them all—was the son-father relationship.

From what Jack has written, though, I doubt whether he is one whose obedience to God will mean his father's enmity. Rather, as is so often the case, he's probably one who can say "father" in easier, more natural accents as he gets more and more practice in crying "Father!"

Thinking about Jack my mind roves back to 1970 when the Greenville College campus, like a good many others, was joyfully overwhelmed by what people were calling "the Asbury revival." Great currents of divine love seemed to be swirling all around us like welcomed spring rains. Spontaneous prayer meetings happened, and amazing sharing times that lasted for hours as person after person stepped to a microphone to affirm new commitment, new joy, new forgiveness, surging new concerns. People came and went from the college church at all hours of the day and night.

Through those awesome days one phenomenon we kept noticing was the eagerness of students to telephone home. There were gladnesses to be shared, confessions to be made, forgivenesses to be asked for. The campus telephone booths were kept remarkably busy, and call after call after call went out from the dormitory extensions. Nearer to God, nearer to the people back home.

One angular young giant especially impressed me. He couldn't wait to get a call through to his preacher father, and to say, "Things are different now, between us!" Then he told the rest of us with choking earnestness that things were *really* different now, all around. Splendidly, joyously different.

What happened at Greenville College during those miracle days in 1970 has happened in other ways at other times all through Christian history: people moving closer to God have found the barriers between them and other people going down, down, down.

Maybe Jack, off in his Texas town, needs to think more about his total Godward response and less, just now, about his frictional father.

Or maybe some words of love, confession, apology, and grace from Jack toward his father are part of the metric motion toward God that he craves, these days, more deeply than he knows.

Twilight deepens. The robin still chweeters. I wonder where Jack worshiped today and what God told him and how well he listened.

21

THROUGH THE DEPARENTING PROCESS

Some time ago the editors of *Christian Herald* magazine asked Dr. James C. Dobson to list and explain what he considers the ten most crucial problems among families today. Dr. Dobson is an eminent writer and speaker on family topics; you may have seen his name often in bookstores or in newspapers. When he prepared his list (as presented in the January 1981 issue of *Christian Herald*), Dr. Dobson listed as his Number 10 item this one: "problems of deparenting." Christian parents, he thinks, find it hard to "deparent" or let their grown children go.

As I read and reread Dr. Dobson's paragraph, I felt like echoing old Archimedes when he discovered the principle of specific gravity and yelled "Eureka! Eureka!" I felt like a British parliamentarian agreeing with a speaker: "Hear! Hear!" Dr. Dobson is so very right. What he calls "deparenting" is a process every family must go through eventually, either peacefully or painfully. On a college campus we watch vivid evidences of it every year as the freshmen arrive, as orientation procedures occur, as Parents' Weekend comes and goes, as we talk with our counselees, as commencements happen.

Sometimes the deparenting is a woeful battleground with dust and blood and trampled turf. Probably it's never totally easy for either the parent or the young person. If both—or either—could ponder from time to time about exactly what the deparenting process has meant up to now and is meaning currently, surely the process could become smoother than when action after action proceeds without reflection.

In your family, between you and your father, how far and how well have things moved in the "deparenting" process? If it has been difficult, are there ways you can help your father cope with it?

The specific ways will, of course, vary from home to home and from one chapter of your life to another. Something that would be a good idea if you are twenty-two might not be a good idea if you are thirty-five or seventeen. Remember what the "Preacher" wrote in Ecclesiastes? "To every thing there is a season, and a time to every purpose under the heaven." A season to be a child totally directed by your parents, a season to be a questing, discovering adolescent guided by your parents, a season to be an adult responsible to your own conscience and to God rather than to your parents.

Not that they're totally put aside, of course. Continuing affection and loyalty and interaction between grown children and their parents can be one of the most beautiful human phenomena to be observed anywhere. (Like the genial retired man I know who recently took his chuckles and his carpentry tools for several hundred miles to help his midyears son remodel a porch. Like parents from California who helped a friend of mine through an Illinois chaos of moving even more recently. Like a man who came back to our town some weeks ago to help his father celebrate birthday number ninety. Like one of my college classmates who is currently spending much of his time and emotional energy caring for his ailing and senile father.)

But what Dr. Dobson calls "deparenting" *has* to happen if you are not going to be an emotionally crippled adult. Surely one of the sadder biographies one can read is that of Edward VII of England whose release into adulthood Prince Albert and Queen Victoria apparently could not cope with, wise though they were in many ways. Perhaps any community has its less famous examples. Do you know a John, never deparented and managing the family business with inner angers in the ways that his father commands? Do you know a George, never deparented and shaping his social life to the whims of his now-widowed mother—who still cooks the kind of breakfast she thinks he should have rather than the kind he enjoys? Do you know an Andrew whose father has always decided which house or automobile Andrew should buy, which clubs Andrew should belong to, how Andrew should vote? (And friends say Mrs. Andrew was not really Andrew's own choice but her father-in-law's nomination.)

Deparenting *has* to happen.

Perhaps for you it has already happened, prematurely and with anguish. As for my young friend Steve, God love him. (I pause to remind myself that a letter to Steve is on my mental agenda, and I ache for him.) When Steve's parents were divorced a few years ago, Steve was evicted from a home into a too-early adulthood. Now the animosity between his father and Steve is like unto the hatred I saw on Arab faces in Jerusalem when a Jewish guide was showing us the Moslem holy sites. If you're a Steve, I hope that various other essays in this book can help you with ideas for going on from here.

If the deparenting is still going on—all twenty thousand episodes of it—how to make it go smoothly and well?

Can you surprise Dad sometimes by making a wiser decision than he thought you would make? Like Luke, who decided last spring he would not go away on a vacation tour with a musical ensemble from his college. Although the tour would have been great fun for sociable Luke, he had a comprehensive examination coming up in his major field, and he knew where maturity pointed. After Luke's father learned about that decision, he would surely be more ready to leave a great many other decisions in Luke's capable young hands. Your daily decisions—about courses at school, summer jobs, how to spend an evening, how to spend a ten dollar bill—will all enter deeply into Dad's readiness to let you fly solo.

Can you let him know from time to time that the parenting of other times, other places, has "taken"? A letter home: "You will like to know, Dad, that I was able to get into the swimming class for my P. E. credit this semester. Most of the guys on my floor are doing cross country or wrestling, but I kept thinking of what you have always said about swimming as a continuing opportunity." "I got the oil changed in the Chevvy yesterday. Remember that talk we had at Grandpa's on my sixteenth birthday about the care of cars?" Or a comment at the supper table: "My roommate's finances are in an awful mess: I'm glad you taught me about using a checkbook, Dad!"

Can you also be overt in your appreciations for trust already extended? Have you thanked him for times when he has permitted you (or invited you, or pushed you) to be an adult? That he chooses you to chauffeur Grandma to the airport when you are seventeen may be, more than either of you know at the moment, a test of your readiness for other ventures in trust for him and independence for you. If you chauffeur well and can be relaxed enough to verbalize a gratitude (a "Hey, thanks for trusting me with the Pontiac, Dad. That was a good experience!"), your gratitude may help to open other doors. Lots of them.

At right times and in right ways, can you be overt in your angers, too?

Solicitous, loving, earnest parents may not know, not realize, how much their clinging and supervising is vexing the now-mature children they should have released into adulthood. If you have been firmly trained in filial loyalties, you may find it very hard to verbalize anger when it happens, but for healing and growth to occur you may need to do some verbalizing.

After a traumatic weekend at home, can you write a calm letter telling Dad that you really must tell him it makes you very angry for him to—to—to what? (What does he do?) To open your mail? To wait up until you come in after social events? To pummel you with advice you haven't asked for? To make appointments for you willy-nilly?

Or can you be calm enough to talk with him face to face and man to man about what in him and in you produces friction and anger?

The frictions may not be instantly removed, of course. But frictions discussed are often frictions more readily resolved. You can be sure he doesn't really scheme and plan now to provoke you to anger! Just to know about the nature and dimension of your anger may be a truly helpful enlightenment to him.

I'm not suggesting the kind of enlightenment that would yell at him in accusations, invective, and sweeping, shrill cries of "You always . . . " and "You never. . . . " Yet even a thunderstorm like that might clear away a good many clouds eventually. It might be better than anger that grows and struggles and writhes inside you when deparenting hasn't happened. And the very process of discussing the frictions may help you toward more of the maturity that will justify and permit the deparenting.

For some young adults the fretful solicitudes of undue and inappropriate continuing parental concern will particularly center on Dad's compulsion to handle your money matters. In our country, in our era, this will be broadly true. And "young adult" may here need to be defined only as younger than Dad rather than in calendar measurements. To Dad, you may still be very young and irresponsible when you are thirty-five or fifty-five. Three days ago I smiled to hear an acquaintance speak several times of a "young" lawyer he knew; I also know that "young" lawyer, and his beard is freely flecked with white.

Now it's quite true that Dad's judgments (at least some of them) may be much better than yours, and you may often want to consult him about investments and expenditures. But deparenting means giving you the freedom to fail, and you will not be fully an adult until you are making your own decisions about your money matters.

A delicate corollary in a good many families will be the dismay it may cause to have Dad keep offering his children gifts of money. ("Huh?" explodes Steve. "Gifts of money? You've got to be kidding. Not *my* Dad! He wouldn't give me enough for a cheeseburger even if he knew I hadn't eaten for three whole days!" Sorry, Steve, but it is still a problem in some families. You have your problems; they have theirs.)

Family differs from family. One father's motivations differ from another father's motivations. Accepting frequent monetary gifts may be a mature happiness for you, or it may be one more part of the incomplete deparenting, an evidence that Dad doesn't really believe in your adulthood and is trying to keep you under his control. How you respond to the gifts will help him in understanding your maturity and will help you in growing into more of it. Depending on circumstances and on the fine tuning of your emotions, you may decide to send back a check ("Thanks loads, but we really don't need it right now") or put it into a special savings account you may label "Inheritance" or buy yourself a pleasant gift you wish Dad had taken time to shop for or endow a Salvation Army project and let him know you did so.

Another aspect of the deparenting. Sometimes mothers go through more durable pain and stress than fathers do in this whole process. Obviously the quality of your relationship with Mom will make enormous differences, and subtle differences, in the quality of your relationship with Dad all through the deparenting times.

Things will go more smoothly for all of you if you can pause now and then to realize that your parents are living through a time of great stress for them, if you can be imaginative in sharing their stresses vicariously, if you can give thought to *their* emotional needs as well as to your own. They need your deep understanding, your creative empathy. They will need reassurances of your continuing love (adult love now, to be sure; not childish love). And they will be glad for reassurances that you are indeed an adult when they learn of tasks you have taken on for an employer and carried through successfully, or of duties you have accepted and fulfilled in church or community.

Deparenting isn't easy, Dr. Dobson says. Indeed, it is not. But your alert and sensitive maturities can make it far easier and far more effective than it might otherwise be.

Primitive societies had their rituals when "boy" became "man" through vigils in a forest or battle with another tribe or stalking lions. You do not have the code of a tribal ritual like that to assert "child no longer" and "ready for a man's roles." Yet intelligence and courtesy and grace can help you, within your parental home and as you move out from it, to devise the rituals that one family will need.

22

YOU AND BIFF LOMAN

Yesterday I talked with a class of sophomores about Arthur Miller's poignantly powerful play *Death of a Salesman*. Have you read that play recently? Have you been able to read it objectively enough to see some parallels that might exist between you and Biff Loman? Would your sympathies for and dismay with a fictional Biff Loman provide some useful perspectives for real-life *you*?

Biff seems real-life enough to arouse sympathy, pity, dismay, disgust, anger, and yet other emotions. As you may recall, Miller gives us a complex account of interacting family members. Biff, now thirty-four, is a perpetual fumbler. At seventeen he had been on the verge of a football scholarship to three universities and of a bright career. He gave up, though, on a prerequisite summer of make-up math—and on essentially everything else in life—after he stumbled upon his salesman father's liaison with a trivial woman in Boston.

Few scenes in any literature, surely, carry more genuine pathos than Biff's incredulous shock when he finds the woman with her giddy laughter and her silk stockings and her black slip in his father's hotel room.

Reading the play again with my present class, I must see Biff Loman, more than I ever have before, as a representative of all disillusioned sons, from old Noah's boys right down to the teen-agers on tomorrow's police reports. Not all of them have known a sudden, stunning jolt like Biff's. Not all have tumbled into such quagmires of disillusionment from such habitual heights of loyal admiration. ("You nervous, Biff, about the game?" Willy had asked before a championship playoff at Ebbets Field. "Not if you're gonna be there," Biff had answered.) Yet there are parallels.

Today after I had marked up my textbook and made a heap of notes for the next class discussion, I sat nibbling my pen and thinking about all the wrong moves that poor Biff made after his private earthquake had dazed him, about how he typifies what anyone may do if/when a father steps or stumbles off a pedestal.

And fathers just don't stay on pedestals forever. Fathers forget promises. Fathers make erroneous judgments. Fathers have limited knowledge. Fathers are erring mortals capable of faults and blunders and sins. To discover their fallible mortality may be exceedingly painful, even when it isn't as horrendous and traumatic as Biff's discovery was.

For example: Of her famous news commentator father Walter Cronkite, Kathy Cronkite told a newspaper reporter that she "hated him" when she "realized he wasn't perfect." (I'm looking at the Washington *Post* for March 11, 1981.) In her book *On the Edge of the Spotlight*, the article continues, Kathy told of remembering vividly the first time she knew him to be wrong, when she had been studying about dolphins and heard him giving flawed information in a dinner conversation. Somewhere between Kathy Cronkite's small rage over imperfect dolphin lore and Biff Loman's avalanches of disillusioned anger stand many of the rest of us at one time or another. What happens next inside us may be crucial to the healing or crippling of our lives.

From fictional Biff—who is so brilliantly depicted that he may seem more real to us than the neighbors and cousins we have known all our lives—we can watch a whole series of inept and fumbling and faulty responses. His father had been wrong, horribly so, but again and again Biff chose destructive responses to his father's failings. Would it be useful to you if you, too, would nibble on a pen for a while, with *Death of a Salesman* in front of you? Are there parallels sometimes between Biff Loman and you?

What about Biff? Well, let's enumerate.

1. He confided in no one. Anger and hurt had festered inside him, we realize, for seventeen years, but apparently he had never told anyone anything.

His good friend Bernard reminisces about sensing a dire change in Biff and being puzzled. ("I knew he'd given up his life.") But Biff had not confided. Rather than talking things over with Bernard, Biff flailed at him. ("We had a fist fight. It lasted at least half an hour. Just the two of us, punching each other down the cellar, and crying right through it.")

Evidently no high school counselor ever knew why Biff gave up his university aspirations, and no clergyman was ever allowed to catch any glimpses of the wreckage inside his soul.

(And you: are you growing through some appropriate confidings?)

2. He reacted in anger.

Reminiscing, Bernard reports a poignant, powerful episode. The pain of it almost seems to scorch the page as one reads. Biff took his prized University of Virginia sneakers to the cellar and burned them in the furnace. The incineration destroyed more than university sneakers; it destroyed a part of Biff, too. Not to achieve became for him a spiteful weapon against his father, a continuing vengeance.

3. He refused to do long-range thinking.

Stunned by what he had learned in Boston, Biff wasn't willing or able to establish goals for his life and work toward them. He drifted from job to job for seventeen years, aimless and indecisive.

4. He did not form or find strong new motives for achieving when the master motive of pleasing an idolized father collapsed.

5. He let his resentment and wrath against Willy burn and burn and burn inside himself. Justifiable anger? Yes, anyone would say so. But retaining it scorched the inner walls of the heart that held it and kept right on scorching. And Biff shriveled. Inside himself he blamed and resented and accused, and those emotions darkened all his life.

The human spirit can experience great *pain* and grow through the process, but *anger* devastates and destroys. It happened within Biff. Is it happening inside you?

6. He did not forgive.

Could he have forgiven? Not easily. Not without the superhuman enablings of Grace. But is any forgiving outside the outer boundaries of Grace?

7. He did not respond to Willy's awkward attempts at reconciliation.

This we know only in part and by guess. The flashback scenes give us mere glimpses of the seventeen desecrated years. "It's when you come home he's always the worst," Mrs. Loman tells Biff as she puzzles about her husband's darkening moods.

On the terrible night in Boston Biff goes sobbing from his father's hotel room, and our sympathies are totally with him. Yet there is a deep pathos, too, in the stage direction: *"Willy is left on the floor on his knees,"* and we realize that Biff has not been hearing the anguished need in his father's appeals.

8. Biff permitted himself a pervasive attitude of having the right to hurt others because he himself had been so deeply hurt.

The playwright's powerful imagination endowed Biff with many winsome qualities, too, but from his first appearance on stage until the final curtain he is prone to say lacerating words. He lashes out and lashes back. His tongue can be a savage weapon. He's painfully skillful in using the snarl and the sneer.

9. He does not face, ever, the realization St. Paul affirmed in Romans 3:23, "For all have sinned and come short of the glory of God."

Willy's sin was great, yes. But if Biff could have seen it as one

more manifestation of the primal contamination that has touched all
human beings since Eden, he would not have needed to stay for
seventeen condemning years in the stance of his initial horrified outcry: "You fake! You phony little fake! You fake!"

If he could have realized, and helped Willy to realize, that sin is
the very stuff for redemption to work on—well, then, he would have
been a different Biff, and we would have a different play before us.

In a way it's always fruitless to pose the "what if" question about
fictional characters; they are what the novelist or poet or playwright
causes them to be. But "what if" can be fruitful when it holds a mirror
up to our own selves, our own deeds, our own attitudes. In the Biff-
mirror, do you read a new reminder—for your now-environment—
that *all* have sinned and come short of God's glory? That our bad
temper and bad manners and bad behavior are also to be identified as
"*sin*"?

10. He did not grope his way Godward during human
calastrophe.

Yesterday I had a query on the chalkboard, among our other
discussion topics, that we didn't get to discuss; maybe we'll come back
to it next time. *How*, I asked my sophomores, *do these people show their
distance from a meaningful faith*? They know the divine Name to use in
profanity, and they invoke it rather constantly against each other in
their hurts and their angers, but the idea of a caring heavenly Father to
whom one can take one's desperations is utterly absent. Hymns and
prayers and biblical promises would be more foreign to them than
Peruvian folklore or African dialects. They're practical atheists, living
with each other as though God does not exist.

(And you, in your desperations: does he exist for you?)

Obviously it's easier, far easier, to analyze a Biff Loman than to
see our own moral selves in any mirrors. What he did we need not do,
if we can be clear-eyed enough to *see* and courageous enough as we
do.

With all his negative stumblings Biff Loman did stumble—or was
pulled by his agonized emotions—into one reaction that differed from
his other responses. As the play moves toward its conclusion, Biff is
driven to the therapy of facing reality. "We never told the truth for
ten minutes in this house," he tells Willy, and in a cold fury he faces
his own limitations: "Pop, I'm nothing. I'm nothing, Pop. Can't you
understand that? There's no spite in it any more. I'm just what I am,
that's all." Sobbing, he clings to his father, and Willy responds in
amazement: "Isn't that—isn't that remarkable? Biff—he likes me!"

Biff's tortured, tangled love for his father has finally been expressed. Honesty has taken over. And, significantly, it comes out as

anger against himself, as confession, rather than as recrimination against Willy. The stage action tells us that Willy, responding, "is choking with his love."

I do not want to read more into the reconciliation than is there. The final outcome of the play is still somber and horror-touched. Yet deep human principles echo and echo in the reader's mind. Truth-telling was retroactive. Spoken-out truth, though voiced in pain and anger and confusion, conveyed its measure of healing and reconciliation. Now, instead of accusing Biff of having ruined his own life for spite, Willy "cries out his promise": "That boy—that boy is going to be magnificent."

(And you. Are you speaking out in truth? Are you uttering the painful confusions of your limitations?)

Death of a Salesman is fictional, I would reiterate, but it is also deeply true. Can the truths built into it help you in the building of your immortal self? And help you now? I hope so.

23

YOUR OTHER—AND UNFAILING—FATHER

The people, recorded Matthew, were "astonished" when Jesus ended the "sayings" we know as the Sermon on the Mount. Matthew's participle stirs the imagination: astonished. Can you visualize widened eyes, tensing knuckles, bearded fisherman faces slack-jawed with amazement? Can you see Peter elbowing Andrew, asking startled questions with quirking eyebrows and eloquent motions of his calloused hands?

One of the ingredients in their astonishment at Jesus' voice of authority, surely, was the amazing assurance Jesus was giving them that Jehovah God—the awesome Yahweh of the Old Testament—was to be thought of as "Father." Reach for a New Testament and a marker pen and review Matthew 5 to 7. What do you notice? Phrases like "That ye may be children of your Father"; "thy Father which seeth in secret"; "your Father knoweth what things ye have need of." There are various other "Father" sentences, among them the pattern prayer Jesus taught to his disciples: "Our Father which art in heaven."

The concept of God as a Father was not unknown among the writers and people of the Old Testament, but the affirmations of it were proportionately few. (Spend a few minutes with a concordance. What do you see? God's voice to David in Psalm 89:26, "He shall cry unto me, thou art my Father." His promise to Solomon through David, in 1 Chronicles 22:16, " . . . and he shall be my son." The inclusive assurance of Psalm 68:5, that God is "a father of the fatherless." The wording, too, of Isaiah 9:6 and Isaiah 63:19b.) A few glimpses. But now the young rabbi Jesus was talking with an outdoor throng in a startling new way about "your Father," "your Father," "your Father." He made it a preeminent theme.

Notice further: in his other teachings and prayers and earthly life events, the Gospels tell us, Jesus often spoke of or to God as "my Father." But in these mountain sayings (Matthew 5 to 7) he used that phrase only once, in Matthew 7:21. In the pattern prayer he told his "astonished" hearers to invoke "our Father." But all through the sayings he kept reiterating "your Father," "your Father," "your Father," with an indelible emphasis.

How well the fishermen-listeners and the other earliest Christians listened to Jesus' sayings is evident in any concordance. (Romans 1:7; Ephesians 3:14; 1 John 3:1; many other passages.)

"So?" says Jerry or Kent or George—or one of their embattled sisters. "So what does all that mean to *me*?"

A great deal, my dears. A very great deal.

Whatever the failings of your human father, whatever the disillusionments that have come to you through his fathering ways (or through his nonfathering ways), you have another Father who is utterly reliable, absolutely unfailing, always with you. And your relationship with the unfailing Father is ultimately the most important fact of your existence; it has to be. Furthermore, it has a bearing upon every other relationship you ever form or have formed or will form, including the one with Dad.

All that being true, could you begin a new era in your life if you would affirm it continually? Could you say to yourself immediately upon awaking, and while you are drowsing away to slumber, and about a thousand times between, "God is my Father!" "God is my Father!" "God is my always-present and unfailing Father"? Perhaps it would be useful for you to get a distinctive marker pen (turquoise? green? purple?) and mark up all the passages you can find in your Bible that declare it: "God is my Father!" Perhaps you would like to acquire a little loose-leaf notebook and transcribe into it poems or conversations or sermon quotes that affirm it: "God is my Father!" And soon you may want to be adding some journal jottings about episodes when the Father lets you know in precious and personal ways that he is indeed *your* Father.

We might note first that he is a Father to whom you can tell anything—absolutely anything—and know that he understands utterly. Yesterday's goof at the office. This morning's anger that burned and simmered, that you loathed even while it happened. The hurts that other people fling against you so casually and carelessly. The inky-dark stains still permeating your conscience from some long-ago partying. Hopes. Trepidations. Needs. Whatever. He is a Father who hears and cares.

And he forgives.

Jubilant news for erring mortals! He forgives!

Turn over to 1 John 1 and let it ring through your being like bells from a carillon. "That your joy may be full," he forgives. And—note this well—he keeps on forgiving. My scholarly Greek teacher, Miss Ruby Dare, wanted us to be very careful with our verb tenses while we translated. In the Testament I'm now looking at, the last verb in 1

John 1:7 is triple-underlined: *cleanseth*. He keeps on cleansing. As we keep needing and telling him our need, he keeps on cleansing. (More bells from the carillons.)

Notice, now, that the forgiveness aspect of God's fathering has very important connections with something we have talked about earlier: one way to honor your human hard-to-honor father is to forgive him. You see, *being forgiven* is always and inextricably linked to *forgiving*. Turn back to Matthew 6. Too often we mutter through the prayer our Lord taught us as though we were so many green-feathered unknowing parrots, but when we truly hear it, the prayer is like high-voltage wires, like emotional dynamite charges. "Please forgive us, as we forgive." Will it help sometimes to amplify it? "Please forgive me for my stupid anger yesterday—and my crummy failures today—as I forgive Dad for last weekend. . . . "

Forgiveness is always a strange and wonderful kind of emotional chemistry. *Receiving* it enables one to give it; *giving* it enables one to receive it. Can you come back to this principle often when Dad has disappointed you, angered you, ignored you, rejected you? Your heavenly Father's message is constant: "While I am forgiving you, I set you free to forgive him; while you are forgiving him, you enable me to keep on forgiving you."

Would it be good to probe, sometimes, about things for which both your earthly father and your unfailing Father need to forgive you? Childhood tantrums? Teen-age flauntings? Blunders in decisions? Faulty judgments toward Dad? To be cleansed by both human and divine forgiveness can really ring the joybells within your own capillaries and up among the archangels. (And if a human forgiveness is for some implacable reason refused to the asker, we can be sure that Heaven's understanding encompasses the whole circumstance.)

He's a listening Father. He's a forgiving Father. What else?

Sustaining, surely. Strengthening. One who is with us in our daily pressures. (Have a look at 2 Corinthians 1:3-4, at the Psalms, at the end of Ephesians 3.)

He's a Father who will help us keep all our other relationships in perspective and proportion if we let him. If the Father means enough to us, then no mortal person will mean so much to us that we'll be emotionally crippled. There's a verse—ah, yes, Colossians 3:5. St. Paul spoke of "inordinate affection" in his extermination lists. "Inordinate affection" can still be viciousness and venom among human beings.

In very fact, do the kinds of pain and anger and dismay we have been talking about all through these discussions sometimes have their rooting in the "inordinate affection" of a young person for a parent? Like Shakespeare's Juliet in another sort of loving, do young people sometimes love their parents "not wisely, but too well"? Recently, while he was pondering about some thoughts like these, a wise man of my acquaintance wrote to me of his conviction that once we rest in God's "all-sufficiency," "our relationship with our earthly father ceases to be the be-all and end-all of our lives." For some persons you know, has Dad's love and approval been too nearly "be-all and end-all"? For them—indeed, for all of us—to be in full harmony with the Father can help in all of our duets with a father.

I would not wish to suggest in all that we have been saying that the Father whom Jesus told his fisherman followers (and us) about is a mere pampering and sentimental benevolence. He is holiness. He is utter truth. He is glory and effulgence and splendor and power. Someone has quipped with keen insight that most of us really want a Grandfather in heaven rather than a Father. He is a Father who will—and must—discipline us for our own good, for our eternal good. When the disciplines come, can we be obedient and not renegade?

Again I visualize a mountain in ancient Israel. Again I hear a young rabbi telling his astonished audience about God as their Father. Can you open your mind a day at a time to be continuously astonished by the same wonderful news? Whatever your human father is or is not, you have an unfailing Father. Talk with him. Love him. Respond to him. Accept his forgivings, his chidings, his disciplines. Accept his instructions about the other people in your life, and especially his instructions about Dad.

Other people will come and go in your life. Circumstances will change. But you always have an unfailing Father.

24

RÉSUMÉS, REMINDERS, REALISMS, REACHINGS

We have probed in a good many directions during all these discussions. Have you been growing as we have talked together? Have you found ideas to plant in your mental seedplots and let sprout there? Have you harvested some suggestions to pass on to a buddy, a roommate, a brother, a cousin whose autobiography is different from your own? Have you been marking up the margins of these pages with dialogue, queries, reactions, repartee?

Back at the outset of our talks I urged you to be thinking hard and experimenting and interviewing the people you trust about how you can honor your father. How has it been going? Have you ventured on some new experiences, new attitudes, new approaches? Did you decide to keep a little journal of what is going on in this department of your life?

I promised you, too, that I would eventually come up with some specific suggestions to put into your hands about honoring the dishonorable or the one who is so very hard to honor. By now, would it be useful to skim back through other topics we have discussed and pull together some résumé remarks? And to add some varied ideas for your possible use? Here's a miscellany to consider. Which of these remindings and reachings might you find useful? Which will stimulate you to think of others I haven't mentioned? Want to reach for a pen and check some items to discuss with yourself in depth? And some to assign yourself for action very soon?

___ 1. The deepest, truest honor you can give your parents is to make valid, wise decisions.

___ 2. It is not real honor to a father for a son to be a puppet.

___ 3. Have you taken your father out for a meal lately?

___ 4. Reporting to him your small (or large) daily successes and achievements brings him valid honor.

___ 5. To apologize to him after specific events or episodes or attitudes may be crucially needful.

___ 6. To keep silence among your friends about his weaknesses or faults or peccadilloes may be a genuine and worthy honoring.

___ 7. Do you sometimes tell your friends with valid pride about his achievements? His long-ago achievements, his recent achievements?

___ 8. In conversations at school or work, do you sometimes quote with admiration from his wit, his aphorisms, his puns, his anecdotes?

___ 9. Are you reminding yourself often that "to honor" may be "to forgive"?

___ 10. When did you last send him a postcard from a trip? Or from an affection?

___ 11. How recently have you thanked him for some years-ago solicitude he showed, some gift he gave?

___ 12. When did you last ask yourself earnestly about your father's present emotional needs? About what *he* may need from *you* during his present life?

___ 13. Do you have a good photo of him in your bedroom? In your office? In your wallet?

___ 14. Do you frequently invoke for him what Catherine Marshall has called "the prayer of joyous blessing"?

___ 15. Do you ask his counsel sometimes in the areas of his expertise? (Income tax, real estate, cars, landscaping?)

___ 16. Are you making progress with candid acceptance of the unpleasant realities—with all that honest acceptance means and will mean in your life?

___ 17. When did you last send him a clipping or a cartoon or a book that he might enjoy?

___ 18. Are you doing deliberate and valiant battles with grim ol' Self-Pity whenever that enemy comes prowling?

___ 19. Is your prevailing attitude "I love him" rather than "I would love him more if he were a nicer person"?

___ 20. After a quarrel do *you* make the overtures of reconciliation?

___ 21. Do you tell him as much as he would like to know about your work, your plans, your dreams? Do you honor him with your confidences?

___ 22. On occasion do you praise Dad warmly in the presence of other persons when you can honestly do so? (For his sales record or his necktie or his barbecue skills or his golf scores? For his *anything*?)

___ 23. Are you becoming brave enough and disciplined enough to tell him quietly that he angers you and how he angers you when he does?

___ 24. Are you appropriately selective in ventilating your feelings? Do you keep between yourself and God (and your journals) the antipathies and angers and accusations that could not helpfully be spoken?

___ 25. Are you finding emotional release through the use of a jotting journal?

___ 26. What have you done with him recently? Fishing? Hunting? Carpentry? Painting? Gardening?

___ 27. Are you accumulating practice in the "soft answer" that diverts wrath?

___ 28. Do you consult with him, when it's appropriate, about your big and little decisions?

___ 29. Have you recently planned a vacation around his preferences for you?

___ 30. When did you last honor your father indirectly by inciting a friend to write to *his* father or telephone or do some other father-honoring deed?

___ 31. What do you call him?—especially when he isn't around? If it's the in thing in your crowd to say "my old man," do *you* retain more dignity? Do you resist your friends' inclination to speak flippantly of a father as "Hank" or "Tom" or "Bill" or "Jim"?

___ 32. Do you sometimes inwardly dedicate to him a difficult task you accept—and then let him know, afterward, of the salute and what it did for you?

___ 33. Do you share with him the praises you receive from professors or bosses or civic organizations? What honors *you* honors *him* also.

___ 34. Do you resist the tendency to ignore him, to pretend he doesn't even exist?

___ 35. Do you thank God explicitly and pointedly for your father's solicitudes or attentions or kindnesses if/when they ever happen? (When he came to see you in the hospital. . . . When he surprised you at your recital. . . . When he sent a greeting for your birthday. . . . When he diagnosed your auto's illness. . . .)

___ 36. Do you keep other relatives informed about his emotional needs as you perceive those needs?

___ 37. Do you telephone him without major incentives? Do you share tiny news items and casual greetings?

___ 38. Are you careful to let him learn about your schedules, your promotions, your plans from *you*, rather than from alumni bulletins or a second cousin twice removed?

___ 39. Do you remember him sometimes with tiny nonsensical no-occasion gifts?

___ 40. Have you enlisted a pastor or other friend to talk in depth with the two of you about the barriers that stand between you?

___ 41. If something good happens to him (a trip, a promotion, a citation), are you his eager press agent? Have you sent local newspapers items about him? Have you let relatives in San Diego and Walla Walla know the news?

___ 42. Have you schemed recently to give him a happy surprise of any sort? (A trip home when he hasn't expected you. . . . A laminated copy of a clipping about you for his billfold. . . . A pen sketch you've made of his boyhood home. . . . Tickets for a sports event. . . .)

___ 43. Are you patiently, resiliently courteous toward his associates whom you must deplore? Do you act with grace when you meet his live-in girlfriend or his newest wife or his drinking buddies? Though not condoning or approving, are you gracious? (Because *you* are honorable, even when he is not. . . .)

___ 44. Do you put people in touch with him who might bring human happiness—or more—into his life? (A former navy chaplain you know who moves to his town. . . . A pastor near him whom you met at a youth camp. . . . Kiwanis acquaintances. . . .)

___ 45. If he chides you, reproves you, pummels you with advice you haven't wanted, are you courteously ready to hear him out? Where his tirades carry truth, can you accept truth rather than just fuming inwardly?

___ 46. How often do you browse among the greeting cards in a drug store and select some little brightness to mail to him?

___ 47. Do you frequently pray about very specific subtopics in the chapters of your filial relationship? (This letter . . . . This visit . . . . This telephone . . . .)

___ 48. Is there family lore or experiences of his own earlier years that Dad would like to tell you about if you'd listen?

___ 49. Do you laugh at his jokes?

___ 50. Do you say "thanks" freely, frequently, and fluently, both for present events and for the boons of early childhood?

___ 51. Are you progressing in veracity inside yourself, and otherwise, to face relationships as they are rather than making false and sentimental pretenses because they're expected?

___ 52. How have you observed his last three birthdays?

___ 53. Do you sometimes salute your parents in some winsome way on *your* birthday—for producing you?

___ 54. Have you recently talked with a pastor or some other trusted friend about any of your least-nice emotions toward your family?

___ 55. Have you thought hard lately about how your father would describe your relationship with him? (Does he perceive you as a father-honoring person?)

* * *

So, how many have you checked? Will you keep thinking about them and experimenting? I hope so. I wonder what other serendipities will turn up, as you let your creativities lead you. As you let Grace lead you.

25

FROM THUNDER, FIRE, AND EARTH-QUAKE

Before we conclude our discussions of your immediate situation, we need to step back through the centuries and look around us. Far more than we usually realize, our present always happens within multidimensional landscapes. Many eras and many places are present in your now.

Will you turn on your imagination and walk back with me through some thirty centuries of recorded human history? Back and back and back.

It's summer and you are an escaped slave and you are living through new experiences that keep you awed and terrified.

Gershom. Maybe your name is Gershom.

You are with a horde of other recent slaves, Gershom. Three months ago thousands of you broke loose from the overseers' whips back in Egypt and followed your leather-hard general out into the Unknown.

Now, with the third new moon since your great escape, you are encamped in rocky terrain at the base of a huge mountain. Accustomed to the flat fields in the Nile delta, you breathe cautiously as you stare at the craggy granite cliffs, the deep ravines, the jutting boulders everywhere. The very air feels ominous, oppressive, expectant. Everyone in the camp is tense, for your general has disappeared somewhere up on the mountain slopes.

Now an alert. The general has come back, and you have orders. All the people are to wash their garments in ritual purification. No one is to touch the mountain now. No scrambling around to explore any foot paths between the boulders or look for wild goats. The death penalty for anyone who puts a toe print on Sinai now. He's to be stoned or hurled to his death. And keep all the livestock from the mountain trails, too, Gershom. (Actually that won't be hard. The general is having official barriers set up.) And pass along the word: no bedding with your wives, anyone, until after the ceremony, day after tomorrow.

What ceremony?

Hair prickles at the base of your skull, and your midriff tightens.

Sunset. Dawn. Sunset. Dawn. Now it is the third day, and your foreboding becomes a blinding terror, worse than anything you ever knew from the slave whips, but mingled with such awe that your very skin seems ready to disintegrate.

Now—oh, look! The whole mountain is wrapped in fire and smoke— smoke as dense as any you ever saw pouring out from the brickmakers' kilns back in Egypt. Suddenly you lurch and gasp. The whole earth is bending and buckling under you. While you totter, someone beside you screams that it is an earthquake. You've never heard of an "earthquake" before, but your feet are as unsteady as they would be on a Nile raft. You feel dizzy and a little nauseated, and strange rumblings are echoing off through all these rocky gorges. A rumbling, grinding noise.

And now, like a crescendo of your own terror but also like a vast unearthly salute, you hear a trumpet. Louder. Louder. Louder. Who has the lung power to blow a trumpet like that?

Then the voice of General Moses. It has to be Moses' voice, although it sounds strange and more intense than you have ever heard it. Then new thunder that is not thunder but a great voice. From the fire, the cloud, the thick mist, a Voice: " . . . no other gods . . . the sabbath day . . . your father and your mother . . . ."

You glance over to see your parents, Dibon and Mara, crouching beside you. Terror is suffocating them, too, as the Voice goes on. Their faces are dough-white, their eyes closed, their bodies as taut as whips.

" . . . adultery . . . false witness . . . you shall not covet. . . . "

The voice has ended. Will It come again? Thunder echoes from the granite crags above you, and you hear some of the tribal leaders begging General Moses to be an intermediary: "You speak to us, and we will hear, but let God not speak to us, lest we die." Immeasurable relief rushes through the mud of your knees. Yes, you breathe, we would die, we would die, we would die.

Another day.

So much happens and so much does not happen that you feel giddy. Moses has been off on the mountain heights, gone for twenty days, thirty, thirty-three, thirty-eight. Your relatives and friends, all these so-recent slaves, have become restless and rebellious. Finally the general's brother has given in to their urging and constructed a visible godling, a golden calf. The people sacrifice to it and make a feast and revel. You, too, Gershom, join in the prancings. You feel a little silly and more than a little uneasy about it all, but the golden calf is more cozy than earthquakes and thunders and having all of Sinai turned into a gigantic smoking kiln.

Wait. Oh, wait. You gasp and cower.

He's back. There's General Moses. And his furious face is like another earthquake, another kiln. He is carrying slabs of stone, and he flings them down in front of him. Crash, crash, crash. His voice becomes a flail thudding across your bending heads. That cozy bull calf is pulverized, and you are made to drink water with calf-flecks in it.

Another day.

You are out near the edges of camp, Gershom, and you see old Moses with a mallet in his hands. He is perspiring as he taps, taps, taps, at a piece of rock. He is smoothing it, chipping the edges. Ah. He is replacing the ones he flung down and smashed.

Early the next morning you watch as he jiggles the slab into his arms, and another slab with it, and starts back up the mountain trail. He climbs slowly, with his brawny big arms straining against the weight. How high will he have to go? Up, and up, and up. He pauses. He moves on again. He pauses. Then the mists intervene, and he is gone.

Another day.

Word ripples through the camp that General Moses is back again, that Yahweh has written words on the new stone slabs. "As at the first writing, the ten words which the Lord had spoken to you on the mountain out of the midst of the fire on the day of the assembly," his tired voice is telling the camp leaders. (Tired, but exalted, too. Resonance and power and a burning, splendid glory are in every word he speaks.)

You are nearer to him than some of the other campers are, Gershom, and you glance from him to Aaron and back to General Moses. The skin of Moses' face looks odd, shiny-odd, as though a little sun were dawning inside his skull. You feel your knees going Nile-mud queasy again. Aaron is frightened, too, you can see, and so are the others. They all back away from Moses in terror. He resists their fright, though, and keeps on talking: "This is the thing which the Lord has commanded. . . . This is the thing which the Lord has commanded." Finally he pauses and lets someone hand him a piece of cloth to drape over his face. You wonder if he is laughing at the rest of you from under that veil, but you think not. Awe would be there, and compassion for the rest of you, but probably not derision. You're glad, though, that he has put on the veil. Now you can think about the ten words that God's finger has inscribed on the stone.

" . . . no other gods . . . the name of the Lord your God . . . commit adultery . . . false witness. . . . "

Your mind spins, Gershom. "Your father and your mother." You watch old Moses, veiled, moving off toward his own tent in the caravan, and you think about Dibon and Mara. Have you honored them, Gershom, on this day in this camp beside the mountain of Moses?

* * *

Slowly I close a leather-bound book, moving markers away from Exodus 19, Exodus 34, Deuteronomy 5. A blue cloth-bound book lies open at Deuteronomy 9.

We are back in our own century now, back from the blazing sun of the Middle East, back from the massive granite cliffs and gorges that modern geographers call Jebel Serbal, Jebel Musa, Jebel Katherina, Ras Safsafa   the mountains of Sinai. And you are looking at me warily.

"So?" you murmur. "What does old Moses have to do with me, anyway?"

A very great deal.

We won't probe all ten of the Ten Commandments just now, but number five will not let us escape. "Honor thy father and thy mother, as the Lord thy God hath commanded thee; that thy days may be prolonged, and that it may go well with thee, in the land which the Lord thy God giveth thee." (I'm looking at the King James Version of Deuteronomy 5.)

You grimace. "Look, that's prehistoric. That doesn't have anything to do with me!"

Oh, but it does.

"Honor your father" is an axis our world spins upon. It's the grain and fiber of all peoples, all cultures, all races. If you could slice through this planet at the equator, you would find it burning there in molten rock. It's in the stars and in the molecules. It's in your corpuscles and in your marrow. It has been a part of your heritage for twenty generations, for all the generations that ever were. It's a basic human equation.

"You really believe that?"

Yes. Yes, I really believe that. If you search folklore and anthropology to find a tribe that has not been parent-honoring, you will find a tribe for which things have not gone well. Parent-honoring; father-honoring. I pause to think for a moment about the legendary ancient Amazons, the warring women who were reported to live only for battle, to take mates only for breeding; they didn't permit the honoring of fathers—and their battle cries were very soon all cried away.

Once in a conversation I mentioned lightly to a friend of mine, a brilliant seminary student, that something or other had to be true because it was in the Bible. "No," he said almost fiercely. "It's in the Bible because it is true!" I don't recall the topic of the conversation, but I remember the intensity of his declaration. Something like that could be said about the Ten Commandments: they are in the Bible because they are verity and reality. They impinge upon our world, upon *us*, because they are verity and reality.

When we live by the Commandments, the whole universe is on our side. When we oppose them, we are opposing the very galaxies and the Maker of the galaxies.

Somebody frowns, and looks about ready to pummel me. Muscles are tight across his jaw. "All that is nice theory," he says with slow, tense agony. "Honor your father, honor your father, honor your father. But I tell you, my father is not honorable. I can't. . . . I can't. . . .

I nod. I reach across to grip his hand. The measure of your pain in estrangement is a measure of what is being violated, isn't it? If a primordial and powerful law of human life weren't being contradicted in your present circumstances, the circumstances couldn't hurt as horribly as they do.

Ancient Sinai is still present to our mortal now, and the Jehovah who issued ancient commands is the still-present Jehovah. He teaches us, as we let him, about the applicability of the commands within our here and now.

I hope all the topics we have already talked about will help you now to find the right dimensions of "honor" within your life. More profoundly, I hope our Lord will guide you into fuller and fuller understandings of what "honor" does and does not imply as it relates to you and the man whose life gave you life.

In ever new ways may you daily know and explore your Maker's will for you!

It has been good to talk with you. For now, good-by. Good-by. Which, being interpreted, is: God be with you!